"The role of a father in our society," says Sara D. Gilbert, "has changed a lot..."

Once he was an aloof, autocratic provider. Today he finds he has a full-time job at home. And one for which he is usually ill-prepared. There are lots of questions about fathering that men are asking and some they should ask themselves before they decide whether they want to be fathers at all...

In this "well-written report on the common vicissitudes of the usual (and sometimes still unusual) models of fatherhood...Gilbert is forthright, forcing the reader to face the reality of everyday life as a father in our modern times."—*American Association for the Advancement of Science*

Sara D. Gilbert

**Visual commentary
by James Stevenson,
NEW YORKER Cartoonist
and a Father**

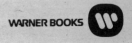

WARNER BOOKS

A Warner Communications Company

WHAT'S A FATHER FOR?

**A Father's Guide
to the Pleasures
and Problems
of Parenthood with
Advice from the Experts**

For Sean's father, and for mine.

WHAT'S A FATHER FOR?

WARNER BOOKS EDITION

Text copyright © 1975 by Sara D. Gilbert
Illustrations copyright © 1975 by James Stevenson
All rights reserved

Library of Congress Catalog Card Number: 74-20992

This Warner Books Edition is published by
arrangement with Parents' Magazine Press

Book design by Milton Batalion

Cover design by Gene Light

Warner Books, Inc., 75 Rockefeller Plaza, New York, N.Y. 10019

Printed in the United States of America

Not associated with Warner Press, Inc. of Anderson, Indiana

10   9   8   7   6   5   4   3   2   1

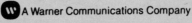 A Warner Communications Company

Acknowledgments

This book, and its author, owe a great deal to a lot of people.

Thanks to Louise Bates Ames, Eda LeShan, Benjamin Spock, and Joyce Sullivan for sharing their wisdom and expertise.

Thanks to Mary Ellen Kulkin for sharing her ideas and the tapes of interviews with "her" fathers (and thanks to Barbara Seaman for introducing her).

Thanks to editor Patricia Coffin for her sharp red penciling, and to Patricia Ayres at Parents' Magazine for her confidence and enthusiasm.

Thanks to Sean and Ian for putting up with it all.

And thanks especially to all the fathers who appear (pseudonymously) in these pages. Their patient and thoughtful answers made the book possible. Hopefully, the questions helped them understand more clearly what a father is for.

Contents

2
WHAT DOES A FATHER GIVE?

3
WHAT'S A FATHER TO DO?

"Daddy's Home!"

"Daddy's home!"

Do you hear that announcement every time you come home from work? If you are like most fathers, you've put in a lot of hard hours before you walked in your front door. And the kind of welcome you receive can sour or sweeten the end of your working day.

Daddy's home! What kind of greeting do *you* get? At our house, here's the way it often goes.

Three-year-old Sean (rhymes with "fawn") wrestles away from his father's hug and punches him hard. "My truck broke! Mommy said you can fix it."

"Later, Sean," my husband sighs. "Right now I want to change my clothes and relax for a minute."

Fathers work hard and get tired.

Women may need to be liberated from household and child-care drudgery, but male chauvinist or not you know from your own experience that a man's everyday routine can be just as tedious and exhausting.

The role of a father in our society has changed a lot

"Daddy's home!"

since the beginning of this century. Once the aloof, autocratic provider, a father now finds he has a full-time job at home, in addition to his office or factory responsibilities.

You are supposed to provide for your family. You are expected to be involved with your kids. And you are presumed to be able to help your wife find free time, too. The way things are, this is a tough assignment. Yet too many experts on family relations and child behavior all but ignore your contribution as a father. It has even been rumored in some circles lately that you are obsolete, Dad.

But you're not—far from it. As we realize the importance to a child of a stable and stimulating home environment from the earliest months of life, and as we acknowledge the need for firm but flexible child guidance in a time of tumult, we become aware that your role is vital.

Still, you are more than just a father. You are also a human being. You need breaks from monotony and drudgery yourself. This book suggests ways to find time for you to be *you*—and to be a better father as well. It proposes a variety of answers to the question: "What's a father for?"

Most of us still expect a father to assume the major financial responsibility for his family. I know I do. My husband changed jobs after Sean's arrival, not for more pay, but to get work with regular hours and more evenings and weekends at home. But that doesn't mean he likes going to the office every morning, or that he is ready for instant involvement when he walks in the door at night.

If you are lucky, you have work that you love, that pays well, and that gives you time that you want with your family. Most men aren't so fortunate. Yet one of the most important roles a father plays is that of being the breadwinner. To make your contribution for the support of your children, you go to work whether you feel like it or not. You may have chosen to be a father, but once you have a child you have little choice but to accept your responsibility—for the next twenty or more years.

We need to do some honest thinking about fathers as

human beings. Men deserve more credit for the sacrifices they make as fathers, for the inevitable problems they must endure. As our society recognizes the needs of women and opens up more opportunities to them, we must explore new ways for both sexes to share the parenting and the breadwinning.

Yet fatherhood is by no means all sacrifices and problems. It has its own special rewards.

Sean watches his father change into loafing clothes and tries his dad's tremendous shoes, giggling and toppling over. He lugs them to the closet and comes back: "Daddy, you're the biggest man I ever saw." We run through the names of other men Sean knows, but Daddy still comes out "biggest."

Fathers are impressive, no matter what sizes they come in.

According to some theorists, a child of any age needs to relate to a soft, comforting figure and to a hard, powerful one for healthy emotional development. In most cultures, ours included, the mother is nurturant, and the father authoritarian.

Today these psychological profiles are overlapping. Still, it is important that you be the "biggest" man your child ever saw. To most men the so-called masculine role comes naturally. But what does "masculine" mean today, and what should ct mean to our children? Answering questions like these requires a new kind of thinking.

My husband lies down to get some rest. Sean jumps feet first on his stomach. From the kitchen I can hear shrieks of joy and groans of mock agony. Then the two of them appear, Sean upside down over his father's shoulder, laughing and protesting.

Fathers can be infinitely more exciting to play with than mothers.

From the earliest months of your child's life, you've been a signal for fun. Did your wife ever complain that the baby's cries sounded like "mama" and that the baby's laughs sounded like "dada"? I did.

The exciting and unfamiliar atmosphere that you bring home with you from the outside world is important for your child's social and emotional development. And the special skills you may ave cone in handy sometimes.

"Now fix my truck!" demands Sean.

"Wait a minute! I want to read the mail."

"NO! I want you to fix it right now!"

Sean is ignored until his whining builds to a crescendo: "Daaaa-dy!"

"Sean! Please stop whining!"

I have been making that request all afternoon, with no success. But for Daddy, Sean stops whining.

Angry, Sean starts kicking the dog. His father's punishment is quick and definite, followed by an explanation: "I love you more than I love the dog, but I cannot allow you to hurt him, especially since you're mad at *me*, not him." Sean scowls but goes to pat the dog.

Fathers seem to swing a little extra authority.

Is it because father is big and powerful? Or is it simply because his discipline is free from the conflicts a mother may feel about punishing her baby? Or is it just the sound of a new voice that makes an impression on the little menace? One of the traditional—and still practical—reasons for marriage is the formation of a partnership for cooperation in child-raising. You may not be that

Crocodiles can't come through walls.

effective a disciplinarian just because you are Daddy, but a harried mother will take anyone's help.

"How come he minds you and not me?" I complain. "He drove me so far up the wall this afternoon that I screamed at him to go to his room."

"You shouldn't scream at my boy," my husband admonishes.

Fathers protect their offspring—even from Mommy.

Since man's earliest days the male has been the defender of his mate and his cubs. You probably won't need to do much physical defending of your children, but your strength and authority are still necessary to fend off frightening monsters—even imaginary ones. When Sean was terrified of the crocodiles in his bedroom, only his father, not I, could convince him that crocodiles couldn't come through the walls.

And a child may need a kind of protection from even the most patient of mommies. Because you are away at work, you can see your children's problems with a perspective that your wife lacks when she has been at home all day.

Modern fathers do a lot more than give mothers moral and financial support in child-rearing. That's one reason for learning all you can about fathering.

Often, of course, your "fathering" is just automatic.

We sit down for supper. Sean starts slurping his milk from a spoon.

"Sean, that's really yukky," protests his father. "I like having a big boy have supper with me, but big boys don't mess with their food." Sean takes one more slurp, then drinks the rest of his milk sedately.

Fathers help children grow up.

Some say a mother's love is absolute, but a father's love is earned. It's by working to earn approval that a child learns to grow. Father's approval is vital to a child's social development.

"What did you do today?" my husband asks Sean.

Sean tells him that he climbed "almost to the top" at the playground, that he made a "biggest" castle and that he talked to grandma on the "telefome" all by himself. His father beams.

Daddies are for being proud.

Your child is pleased when you are proud of him or her. And the pleasure goes two ways. A man is glad to have the opportunity to be proud of his child, since a child is in a way an extension of himself.

Sometimes this attitude goes to extremes, causing complex conflicts within a family. A child may rebel violently against parent-imposed goals, or be stifled by a parent's misdirected pride. A father may use his child as a surrogate to work out his own problems. He may even end up competing with his children. Understanding your role as a father and yourself as a person is important.

My husband wants to talk to me. Sean keeps babbling, thinking up interruptions and reasons for me to leave the table. His father gets exasperated: "Sean, you've had Mommy to yourself all day. Now it's my turn and I want to talk."

"Mommy!" Sean pleads.

Some competition—and even a little jealousy—are normal.

Family competition is important if a child is going to learn to live with other people's conflicting wants and demands. A boy needs (unsuccessful) competition with Daddy for Mommy. A girl needs (unsuccessful) competition with Mommy for Daddy. This promotes a healthy sexual development which doesn't necessarily end with the "Oedipal" stage. Fathers influence the sex identification of their children through adolescence by providing a model as a man and a pattern for the relationship between the sexes. Any such competition can be threatening if you don't keep it in perspective. Nor does the father's importance as a sex model mean that you have to be a "he-man" in the traditional sense.

I'm late for a lecture at the museum, and as my husband clears the table, he asks, "When do I get liberated?"

Fathers get the short end of a lot of sticks.

I ignore the question. "Don't forget his bath—his pajamas are on his chair. He should go to bed around eight."

"I always get him to bed without any fuss. Of course, I wait till he tells me he's ready, so that may make it easy."

"It sure does," I laugh. "Have a good time, you guys."

As I close the door, I hear: "Now, you can fix my truck, Daddy."

Family rules and roles are changing. As more women feel comfortable about leaving home to work, to pursue a talent, or just to enjoy themselves, men are sharing household jobs that previous generations labeled "feminine." Despite initial unwillingness, you may find that helping to care for your kids brings you closer to them.

Our new customs free more than women. As the social structure opens up, you may have the opportunity to change the life-style you were trained for, to "fulfill" yourself in some new role. My husband would rather take photographs than work in an office, for instance. But office jobs pay salaries. So we arrange time for his photography, even though our families and neighbors may think his solo picture-taking trips odd. A father, like a mother, should find ways to satisfy inner needs within the structure of family commitments.

Home from my lecture, I have a report. My husband had tried to fix Sean's truck and couldn't.

"But Mommy *said* you could fix my truck!" he had cried. He'd thrown a tantrum on the floor.

His father, furious, had retreated to the den to sort through some slides he'd taken. "And pretty soon, you know what he did? He came in with me, pouting a little, and watched for a while. Then he said he wanted to do pictures too, just like me. So I gave him some rejects, and he stayed there as long as I did, looking at his slides and rearranging them. He says he wants a camera for himself."

Fathers are for imitating.

A parent's major function is to provide a model for his child. This doesn't mean you want your child to be your mirror, but how satisfying it is when he respects and admires you enough to *want* to be like you.

Girls need to imitate fathers, too, especially now. They need to know that lives are led outside of home and family. Beyond that, you play a large part in setting the tone for your child's future. Your way of life can suggest to your sons and daughters how they can go out into the world and achieve what they want.

That's another reason for a father to create a life that he finds personally satisfying, because when a father is happy with his life, his child will be proud to be like him.

When Sean was finally ready for bed, he had asked his Daddy to read two books and then tuck him in. "No, that isn't the way Mommy does it," he complained.

Kids need mothers, too.

Then, with a hug, Sean had said, "That's all right, you're a nice Daddy."

"That's the kind of thing that makes it all worthwhile," my husband comments.

"But what about the truck tantrum?"

"Oh well, I shouldn't have gotten so mad myself, I guess."

The next morning I ask Sean if he and Daddy had a good time while I was out at my meeting. "Yeah, but he didn't fix my truck."

"Well, daddies can't do everything."

"Why?" he asks.

"What do *you* think a daddy is for?"

"I don't know—I'll have to ask my Daddy when he comes home," and Sean is confident that his father will be able to answer him.

Supreme authority on everything, disciplinarian, role model, playmate, and mother's helper—that's a lot to ask of a man who works all day and needs some time to be himself.

Some evenings, of course, you may have the distinct impression that all you are needed for is paying the bills, and even that may be beyond you. Sometimes Sean's indifference to the cry, "Daddy's home!" is so thick that my husband claims only the dog is glad to see him.

What's a father for, anyway? What made you get into this?

1

WHY IS A FATHER?

"Why was I ever a father? Why was my father ever a father?"

CHARLES DICKENS

1

What Made You Get Into This?

"Why? Why me?!" is a father's cry at times of crisis.

Your wife is in the hospital having twins, and you are in charge of a Terrible Two.

It is 4:20 A.M., your turn to feed, and the burp won't come.

It is the first day of the month after the orthodontist started to work on your son's teeth.

All 500 invited guests come to your daughter's wedding.

Your son has just finished law school and has decided to become a carpenter.

What made you get into this? On the bad days you won't find a happy answer to this mournful question. "It was New Year's Eve and it seemed like a good idea at the time" is little comfort. But in calmer moments, "Why?" is a question worth asking. Maybe you should even have explored your motives before you were inevitably on your way to fatherhood. If you did, good for you, because fatherhood is not a project to be undertaken as an afterthought.

Why *did* you become a father?

25

It used to be that fatherhood was almost inevitable, that is, if you had the healthy physical drives and social consciousness of a normal man. Now, it is not. Contraception is easy, sophisticated, and available. Abortion is legal. Hardly anyone needs a gang of children to help plow the south forty. In fact, it is socially acceptable to have as few children as possible, or none at all.

Fatherhood takes money, time, and energy. It curtails freedom. It pins you down to a minimum of twenty years' work and worry. But men like you still become fathers. Even guys who aren't roped in by marriage are taking on the responsibilities of fatherhood these days. *Why?* Even if you've already sired a baker's dozen, exploring your own reasons for fatherhood will make you a better father.

In asking a lot of fathers, "Why?" I have received answers ranging from, "I think it's a healthy expression of the ego," to "Well, my wife always wanted kids." The "experts" have not been much more scientific. So, for what it is worth, here is a list of motivations, some legitimate and some not-so, for fatherhood.

Search for Eternity?

Science recognizes a reproductive drive in all organisms—the inborn push to keep the species from extinction. Some psychologists surmise that in man this reproductive drive is part of a far more complex and personal survival instinct. Since children represent your only hope of lasting beyond your allotted three score years and ten, your natural drive for survival compels you to grab as big a chunk of the future as you can.

After all, within your sperm cells is a web of genes that stands uniquely for you. Without this magic stuff, a man can feel anxiously mortal; with it, he is "immortal." And men have been searching for immortality since Adam left the Garden. Yet identification with one's vital fluids can go too far.

Do you feel, as a lot of otherwise rational guys do, that to prove your virility you must father a child? For centuries, babies have been evidence of a man's "masculinity." Although nowadays small families are fashionable, it is still hard for people not to wonder whether there's something "wrong" with a man who has *no* children. Many cultures, including our own, equate sexual potency with masculinity, and offspring with sexual potency.

As a case in point, in many instances of possible infertility it is hard to persuade a husband to go in for a relatively simple test until his wife has undergone long exams and nothing has been found "wrong" with her.

Then there's the man who sired a literal baker's dozen, and when, after the thirteenth child, his wife agreed to a hysterectomy to preserve her health, he left her—as if procreation had been his only motive for marriage.

Maybe the very ease of birth control today makes the male procreative urge somehow stronger. The current control that *women* exert over pregnancy—choosing to use or not use pills or diaphragm, to abort or not to—is supposed to have an almost castrating effect on men. The frustration a man may feel at not being able to plant a new baby in his wife's belly at will might intensify his drive to reproduce. This may be one reason some men choose fatherhood.

How much of your interest in fatherhood was a desire to prove your manhood? And how will that affect your relationship with your kids? If your offspring are simply proof of your virility, you are going to treat your children as objects—and that's not what becoming a father is for.

Fatherhood only begins with impregnation. Probably nothing in your genes or hormones forces you to provide for your offspring from obstetrician through college. But this practice does have what sociologist William J. Goode calls a "biosocial base." We are conditioned, whether we realize it or not, to *want* to be parents in both the biological and the social sense. That is, if you were "raised right," you have no choice.

So, whatever your conscious reasons for wanting to become a father, you were probably also motivated by involuntary biological and social forces toward a uniquely human search for immortality. Some men seek eternal survival by trying to make their children exactly what they are themselves or in the image they dream of being.

Maybe you love selling, and already you are training your kids to be the best damn little salespeople in the world. After all, it has given you a good life, and you want at least as much for your kids.

Say you've built up a business or perfected a trade, and you don't want it to die with you. It is natural to want to establish a dynasty to carry on your work—kings have been doing it for centuries. But each child is a unique being, and deserves to fulfill his or her own uniqueness (notice how few kings there are any more). Nevertheless it is amazing how many young people do follow in their father's footsteps today. When that happens, it is the effect of good fathering, rather than a cause for fatherhood.

Some fathers leave only fleeting footsteps to follow.

Take the guy whose hour of glory was as a football star in his senior year at college. Now his only involvement with his toddling son is to teach him to throw a football. At 18 months the kid thinks it's fun, but in ten years he may turn to tiddlywinks to spite the old man.

Perhaps you always wanted to be a doctor or an artist, a senator or a judge. But war, or poverty, or bad luck aborted the dream. Your kids can make that dream come true, can't they? No. A legitimate motivation for fatherhood may be a search for "eternity," and it is an American tradition for a father to hope that his children will do better than he did. That doesn't mean that a father can plug his children into the future to reverse the circuit of his own failures. His children cannot fulfill his hopes for himself.

Why did New York artist Herb Adams want to be a father? He took a long time to answer the question, watching his kids roughhousing in a living room that a moment before had been tidy. "I guess it's the creation of life—I don't mean an extension of myself, a re-creation of me—but the creation of a human life that I can affect."

You agree? You know better than to use your kids as a mirror? But don't you get a happy twinge in your pride gland when someone praises your child as "the spit and image of her old man" or identifies your kids' nimble figures, sharp mind, or broad shoulders with your own?

You don't catch yourself expecting your offspring to enjoy the things you did when you were growing up, or daydreaming about preparing them to take over the business? You don't? Okay, then let's look at your motivation for fatherhood from another angle.

What Does Your Name Mean?

A monologue by comedian Shelley Berman comes to mind. It wasn't meant to be funny. It recounts the time when young Berman broke the news to his father that he wanted to be an actor. "Sheldon," Berman quotes his father, "Sheldon, just don't change your name."

When a child, especially a son, changes his name, he deals an almost literal death to his father. People who change their family names usually have some superfi-

...he'll need to have a nickname.

cially good reason: the name was unpronounceable, "foreign-sounding," "Jewish," bad for business, a cliché. But if you take a closer look, you'll probably find hostility between the son and his father.

How would *you* feel if your son grew up and changed his—your—name? Your reaction may illustrate another reason for fatherhood: "to carry on the name." It's not an explanation expressed in most circles, but don't you have some feeling about not letting the family name "die out"? And why not? You've probably got a family to be proud of.

First names, too, carry burdens. Either the child's personality is expected to echo a name like Patience, Faith, or Victor. Or the child is thought to resemble the friend or relative it was named for. And if you've got a "Junior" in the family, he'll need to have a nickname to distinguish him from the "old block."

It's no sin for a father to want to carry on his name, as long as he doesn't get hung up on expecting something special from his children "because they're Joneses." Sociologists point out that tracing the family name through the male line is a cultural holdover from an earlier and more rigid patriarchal age. This is one reason why men traditionally hope to have sons. Now it is becoming popular for women to keep their own family name in some form when they marry. So if you want your name to be carried on, you don't have to keep trying for a boy—as long as you are a father whose name your children will *want* to continue.

How's Your Old Man?

Is your father's name one that you are happy to have? Or would you rather change it? How did you get along with your father?

Recent studies indicate that a man develops traits of fatherliness—an "empathic responsiveness" to his children—from having had a warm and loving father. An overly strict or cold father may inhibit the fathering instinct. If as a child you had a worthwhile experience with your father, according to psychoanalyst Therese Benedek, you grew up wanting to be fatherly.

On the other hand, a surprisingly large number of the fathers I talked to feel like young New Jersey lawyer George Forrest: "*My* old man? I'd rather forget him." Yet George, like many of the others, is a warm, involved, concerned parent who seems to be enjoying his role. Wanting to be a better father than your own was is another way of reacting to a bad relationship with a distant or harsh father.

Or the subconscious child in you may want to "show" the old man by being an even more rotten father than he was!

Untangling the feelings about the fathering you enjoyed—or missed—can make a big difference in how you treat your children. You owe it to *them* to do a little soul-searching.

Is the Frying Pan Worth the Gleam?

Okay, so we've been digging around in your subconscious. Still, the best reason you have for wanting to be a father is that it was New Year's Eve and having a child seemed like a heck of a good idea at the time. Some men like being fathers more than they thought they would, and some like it less.

"I'm glad my wife pushed me into it," publicity agent Dick Taylor admits. But Bud Kreutz, a father of four with a new real-estate business, had pictured a cheerful rambling house full of kids, dogs, and toys. Now, he confesses, he "stays away from the madhouse as much as possible."

Some guys never wanted to be fathers at all, before or after the fact, and carry out their role with a spoken or unspoken "I-didn't-ask-to-have-you" attitude. With contemporary birth control, these cases should be rare, luckily; because fathers who feel this way have a problem—and their kids have a worse one.

Hopefully, you don't fall into such an extreme category. Still, you do need to keep in mind, as you grit your teeth over the minor and major crises of your life as a father, that whatever *your* reasons and subconscious motivations for fatherhood were, your kids did not ask to be born. So whether the gleam in your eye that New

Year's Eve kindled a glow of paternal bliss in your heart or lit a fire under life's frying pan, your children didn't get you into this. You did it yourself. They and you need to make, not the best, but the most, of the situation.

You Have a Choice

You may not have known what you were getting into the first time around, but you do have a choice about how many more children you want.

An addition to your family is of course something you and your wife should agree upon. In deciding, keep in mind a study that showed what you might have guessed: that a father's disposition goes steadily down as the number of his children increases.

It's not just *your* kids who drive their father crazy—all kids do it. Our society makes tremendous demands on a man, especially a father. As a result, more men commit suicide than women, they die younger, and get sick oftener. And no wonder—we expect a man to earn a good living (and prove his "status" by continually advancing his career), finance the raising of his children, make like a father, emancipate his wife, mow the lawn, and carry out the garbage.

If you want to keep your health and your sanity, you'll think again about crowding the nursery. You'll want to take a good look at your finances and take time to consider your own life goals. You'll try to clear your mind of such irrational goads to paternity as carrying on your name, or keeping up with your father's record. With such careful consideration and planning, each new child will be a welcome individual.

Because it is now possible and acceptable to have a small family doesn't mean you *have* to. But a child should be more than another mouth to feed.

A man's ethnic or cultural background may prescribe a large family. His religious convictions may proscribe contraception. In cases of such strong social pressures, an extended family structure or a supportive spiritual framework helps parents to cope healthily with a large family. Mormon couples, for example, are encouraged to be prolific, but church doctrine sets forth rules for family structure and interaction that make managing a big brood easy.

For most couples, the key word is "choice." You and your wife may have to do some compromising on family size. I once thought I wanted six children; my fiancé got me down to three before he undertook any permanent commitment. Now we find that one may be plenty.

Family planning is one sign of a good father. Research shows what would seem obvious: Fathers who participate

It was New Year's Eve and it seemed like a good idea...

in planning the size of their families tend to be more involved with their wives and children than fathers who leave the decision up to the women or ignore the choice altogether. Wise use of birth control also indicates a concern for your children's future. As one father put it: "My biggest worry is what the world's going to be like when Mike and Jennie grow up." Limiting his family to Mike and Jennie is one way in which he's safeguarding their future.

If you choose the number of children you have, you will be a happier, less anxious man and therefore a better father.

What made *you* get into this?

One young father, a bit embarrassed by trying to express intimate emotions, explained, "I don't know that I had any *reasons* for wanting a baby. It's just that we were so happy—we had found so much love in each other— that we wanted to share it."

It may be possible to answer the question only in hindsight. I talked to many men who had no idea what they would get out of their roles as fathers. They were launched into parenthood because their wives wanted to "quit working"—or "because it was New Year's Eve." They were already in it before they found the answers to the question of what made them choose fatherhood. They found that the rewards seemed to more than outweigh the 4:20 A.M. burps or the carpenter with a law degree.

Once you are in it, try to get the most out of it!

2

What Do You Get Out of It?

Coming home to happy cries of "Daddy!"—hugging, kissing, nibbling, and roughhousing—small children's uninhibited glee is one of the biggest payoffs a father can have. "A kid fits so nicely under one's arm or on one's shoulder."

"Now that my boys are big enough," says mailman Al Foster of his 8- and 10-year-olds, "my greatest pleasure is going places with them, showing them how to do things, watching them explore."

Airline executive Pete Morison's children are nearly grown. "It's funny," he says, "but my reward is knowing that my kids can do without me. I guess I miss being able to hold them, feeling that they worship me, but I'm glad the diapers and screaming are gone, and I'm happy we've all survived as well as we have."

Feeling Better

"Rewards?" One guy I asked was puzzled and annoyed. "If you don't know, I can't tell you. It's just . . . it's just the feelings I have—feelings I don't think I would have had if I hadn't had the kids."

Another father commented, "The few books I've seen that do mention fathers ignore any feelings they might have for their children. It's almost as though fathers aren't *supposed* to have feelings."

In a way, he's right. Part of the traditional Western "masculine ideal" has been "toughness" and "rationality," which are too often equated with a lack of emotion. In sociologist language, the "expressive" dimension is suppressed in favor of the "instrumental."

Most men tend to be inarticulate about whatever feelings they do allow themselves. Maybe they are ashamed to admit emotion. Maybe it is because little boys are less rewarded for overall verbal ability than they are for their more physical and hardheaded skills.

How many times did you hear while you were growing up, "Boys don't cry," and how many times have you said that to your son? I hope not often because, as gigantic football hero Rosie Grier sings, "It's all right to cry." More and more men are realizing that it's all right to feel and express the whole range of emotions.

Still, many fathers seem to feel more comfortable showing their emotions in physical terms. Hugging and roughhousing are "manly" ways of saying "love." Or they express their feeling of being rewarded in terms of pride, an acceptable emotion for men. A father who suppresses his emotions deprives himself of much of the richness of parenthood. One who can open himself up to the feelings his children elicit will be well rewarded.

How sharp is *your* sensitivity? For instance, how did you feel when you first saw your child? Proud? Joyous? Concerned? Relieved? Bored? Frightened? Obstetrician George Schaefer, after many encounters with new fathers, thinks that your initial reaction may provide a clue to the tone of your future relationship with your children.

And can you remember how you felt when your baby first smiled at you? It probably wasn't "just gas"—babies do smile at very early ages, although maybe not at scientists. When that happened, your child was showing that you were to him a trustworthy person. From that trust comes love and the basis upon which you will build all your fathering. If you can open yourself up to that first smile and all that follows it, you can reap the real, if inexpressible, rewards of fatherhood.

Headaches and Hero Worship

Well, all this misty-eyed nostalgia about the pleasures of parenthood is fine, you say, but fatherhood can be a pain, too. Of course it can.

You've got a new baby in the house. Your wife is tired, cranky, and preoccupied. It looks as though your sex life never came back from the hospital. In honor of the new arrival, your older child has forgotten all about toilet training and is leaving messy pants and puddles all over the house. What's more, you'd swear that the baby cries by the clock, every quarter hour. You've just dozed off after the midnight feeding, brooding about your 9 A.M. meeting, when suddenly an unearthly scream comes from the baby's crib. You end up with the little one, because your wife has to reassure its terrified sibling that monsters have *not* attacked. You're terrified yourself. Obviously something is the matter—the baby is in real pain. But a half an hour later, after you've walked and rubbed and patted, up comes a big burp and a lot of gas and the baby is contentedly asleep on your shoulder.

Or there's the time your 8-year-old just missed being hit by a car while riding his bike on the street you had forbidden. You could have killed him yourself.

Or the night your teen-aged daughter was out with a strange-looking character in an even stranger looking sports car and didn't come back on time. As it got later, your adrenalin level rose with worry so that when she walked in the door, safe and sound, with some trifling excuse, your anxiety turned to anger and you raged.

Where's the payoff for headaches like those? The very intensity of the alarm you felt when the baby screamed, the bike toppled, and the night grew later only proves the great value you place on your children, and your close ties to them. And it is rewarding to be the great big scratchy creature who took the baby's pain away, the 8-year-old's boss who was right after all, or the father of the teen-ager who is glad the main man in her life worries about her.

37

"Part of the subjective reward for father—the payoff if he does his job well—is a certain inimitable fatherly feeling. . . . This is quite a different sense of identity than is characteristic of . . . motherhood. It is a consciousness of being the provider, the cornucopia figure, the 'big daddy,' the dispenser of largesse (gifts, money, pardons, knowledge): the source of all good things, and wisdom, too," writes sociologist Leonard Benson.

Or as George Forrest put it, "because of the way the kids react to me, home is the only place I feel like a king."

"I'll have to ask my Daddy about that," is my Sean's response to any question he can't answer.

Now, maybe you'd rather *not* have to answer all those questions. You understandably might *not* always enjoy having a scruffy little kid blow hot breath on your knees while you're trying to fix a faucet, or squeeze beside you into your chair with a book when you'd planned to read the paper.

To your kids, for a time at least, you are a combination of Superman and Santa Claus. Later your teen-agers will let you know in little ways that even though they do consider you an antediluvian subhuman tyrant, they do depend on you. Having someone look up to you or lean on you can make you feel a little taller. Hero worship is good for any father's ego.

But there's an even richer payoff. All those questions you took time to answer, all the faucets you could have fixed better alone, all the stories you read instead of the

Your daughter was out with a strange looking character in an even stranger looking sportscar.

paper, all the tantrums you coped with, all the rebellions you survived—all the real and figurative headaches you suffered—helped to process the raw material of genes and pee into an honest-to-goodness human being.

Developing Raw Material

That is probably the overriding reason why most men are glad they became fathers. After all the deep psychological motivations and biosocial bases are unearthed and reburied, we're left with: "The baby started out as nothing, and I helped make her into something." Children can give purpose to life; helping them grow brings personal satisfaction in an increasingly impersonal world. One father who has adopted his children commented, "I didn't 'create' my babies, but I am creating my children's personalities, and that's exciting." In sociologist William J. Goode's words, it is "spectacular," turning a "squawling blob" into a human being. A lot of that is *your* doing, Dad.

Processing raw material is different from re-creating someone in your own image. And it's harder. It takes getting to know yourself *and* your children. It takes learning when to step in, when to stand back; when to praise and when to punish; when to tighten the reins and when to leave them slack.

Pride in one's work makes the work worthwhile. Good fathers deserve to pat themselves on the back. You may not use your children as a mirror of yourself, but the people they grow into are a reflection on you as a father.

Your Kids Can Teach You a Lot

"Yeah, I think I'm getting to be a pretty good father," allows George Forrest, "but I've learned how from my son—Mike has taught *me* how to relate to *him*." For George, whose relationship with his parents was "a textbook case of what *not* to do," the "lesson" in loving that his 3-year-old has given him is sufficient reward.

You may be "big daddy," dispenser of wisdom, but your kids are wise in their own way. Herb Adams enjoys spending time with his children "because of the things they *see!* Their minds are unfettered by "oughts" and "of courses." They can turn your head around with their own kind of imaginative logic, and the world becomes a simpler place.

One little boy in our neighborhood was asking about a war documentary his father was watching. "Well," he concluded, "if somebody wanted to fight *me* like that, I'd just spank them and tell them to go back where they belonged."

A father was chastising his misbehaving offspring. After cataloguing the evils the child had committed, and the reasons against each of them, he said, "I just don't

A combination of Superman and Santa Claus

know what else to say." "Well, Daddy," he was advised, "you could say 'I love you'."

At every age they ask questions:

"Why did they dig that hole, Daddy?" "Why is the bottom half of my shadow bigger than the top?" "Why do we make babies, Daddy?" "Why can't ladies be garbagemen?" "Why are white people richer?"

And you have to answer them—with an answer, if you have any self-respect, that you've thought about. In thinking about things you haven't considered in a long time, if ever, you learn, Dad.

As your kids grow into adolescence, they may seem to amass great wisdom. It may be tough to take it that they think more of themselves and less of you than was the case when they were little. Anthropologist Margaret Mead said of the youths of 1969 that they were the "first generation born into a new country." That applies to every new wave of youth. Pollster Daniel Yankelovich reports that a "social generation" now spans only seven years, not the traditional twenty. If customs, tastes, and concerns change every seven years, parents may indeed need to keep in touch with several generations.

Today's young fathers express confidence that they will be more flexible than their own fathers were in tuning into the future through their kids. Maybe one thing is sure, the fathers will know *themselves* better by the time their kids are adolescents.

Fathers Grow, Too

Before you had a child, you may have believed in the myth of the "grownup." Having put in the required number of years and attained the maximum height, you may have felt that you did belong by right in that long-legged world you'd always looked at from the other side. Then you became a father. You found yourself being placed in the role you'd always reserved for *your* father. And you may have found, like many, that you didn't really feel like the all-knowing giant your child made of you. People probably don't ever grow *up*, but they do keep on growing. Your kids can help you grow, if you let them.

"I find that since the kids have been born, I'm more patient than I ever thought I could be," one father says. "My temper hasn't evaporated, but it didn't seem fair to inflict it on the babies. Now it's a habit—it even carries over into work. I can put up with a lot more than I used to."

"Children are excellent emotional barometers," insurance agent John Green points out. "They sense feelings in you that you aren't aware of, and they make you see them. My Joe says, 'Why are you getting so angry, Dad?' And I realize I *am* angry, though I wasn't admitting it. Then the question is 'Why?'—and when I figure it out, I've changed a little. The emperor has no clothes. . . ."

Another father finds he has actually begun practicing what he preaches to his kids. "It's impossible to keep saying 'share', 'do unto others,' 'waste not, want not,' 'pick up your clothes'—without beginning to take it seriously!"

Just keeping your senses open is rewarding. Herb Adams enjoys being a kid again, doing the things kids like to do. "Hell," he says, "it's just plain fun."

So you can get a lot of your father role—physical pleasure, emotional response, ego gratification, pride in creative craftsmanship, personal growth, and "plain fun." "I never knew that something so small could give me so much," John Green said about his new child.

But what about all you've put *in*? "The baby's cute now, but wait till it grows up—will it be grateful? Not a chance!" an older man warns.

Save Money, Not Kids, for Your Old Age

Is gratitude a necessary reward for fatherhood? "No" is easy to say. It is easy to nod "amen" to "after all, the baby didn't *ask* to be born." A friend's father bemoans the fact that he gave his sons the best of everything and now they've "gone off to do what *they* please." We shake our heads, "Tsk, tsk! What a rotten father"—but put yourself in that father's place.

You've shelled out thousands, maybe hundreds of thousands, to feed, clothe, doctor, and school your children. You've worn yourself out in a job that was steady but far from exciting. You've forgone new cars, evenings out, and trips away because of things your kids needed. After all that, might *you* not be tempted to gnash your teeth at the ungrateful brats who are off "doing what they please?" You might just be tempted.

Maybe *your* offspring will give you considerably more than an occasional hello when you're doddering. A surprisingly large number of elderly parents do live with their children. Even more receive financial help from them. But as you well know, costs are so high these days that the younger generation can barely take care of itself, let alone its parents—and things won't be any cheaper when you're 65. Not only that, we are an increasingly mobile nation, and you may need an itinerary to keep track of your grown children and grandchildren. So it seems wiser to count up your retirement benefits and social security than to count on your kids.

...you might get a late-night note——

If you have been a warm and open parent, it is more than likely that your children will help or at least keep in touch. They'll be willing to, that is, if their father hasn't spent their childhood ringing up his sacrifices on his mental cash register, and hinting pointedly for the payoff in gratitude. Save money, not kids, for your old age.

Of course, you are a modern parent with no plans to be dependent on your children. Still, you may agree with one father's complaint: "My kids don't know *how* to say 'thank you'." Your children may never "thank" you for your fathering. It may, frankly, be enough that they don't curse you. But someday, after you've become a grandparent, you may get a late-night note from your son or daughter saying: "Now I know what it's all about. I hope I can be as good a parent as you were."

If you raise your children wisely and warmly, your satisfaction won't be in their "gratitude," but in the fact that they *are* off "doing what they please," and that you made it possible.

2

WHAT DOES A FATHER GIVE?

"Most men seem to want to be good fathers, but many...do not seem to be aware of what functions they can perform beyond being providers."

HENRY BILLER AND STEPHAN WEISS

3

What Makes a Man a Father?

The functions that fathers perform have been evolving since humankind began. Fatherhood is a "social invention," Margaret Mead has written. Yes and no. No, if the statement is read as saying that the human family could not have developed without the creation of fatherhood as a social role. Human fatherhood *is* an "invention." That is, men had to "learn," through eons of evolutionary trial and error, how best to insure the survival of their own unique species.

All creatures have had to evolve their own patterns for procreation and survival, so what makes the human father different? Before we answer that, let's go back to the birds and the bees.

Of Birds and Bees

Virtually every animal above the protozoan level needs a male and a female to reproduce its kind. How about that, birds-and-bees freaks?

In many species, the male impregnates the female and is never seen again. Take *Canis familiaris*. Have you ever wanted to file a paternity suit against a neighborhood dog, but were unable to figure out which one gave you nine puppies?

In others, a pack or clan stays together, and though individual males and females may pair off, the male takes little part in the care of its offspring. The lion may be known as the King of Beasts, but it is the *lionesses* in his pride who kill his supper and fight his foe—and nurse his cubs, too. In some cold-blooded families, the male simply sprays semen over the roe and swims away, whereas in others, the male is assigned the task of carrying the eggs around until they spawn. Then he takes off.

Some male birds take turns sitting on the eggs, and carry food to their brooding mates. And we all know about male bees, who serve out their brief time by waiting on and courting a queen.

Among the "lower" animals, the role of the male is biologically determined or instinctually organized. But the fatherly behavior of the human male goes far beyond instincts or biological necessity.

Making History

Recent paleontological and anthropological findings trace the history of that unique being, the human father. Your role, Dad, grew out of a complex of evolutionary events that made *Homo sapiens* possible.

Back more than four million years ago man literally came down from the trees. Life for the earliest protohumans was more complicated than the ape's relatively safe tree-oriented existence. To hunt and fend off the fierce earthbound animals of the age, they had to learn to use sticks and stones as weapons and tools. In order to teach the young members of the clan how to make and use these crude implements, our predecessors developed a rudimentary language. The use of tools and language produced greater intelligence. As a result, the hominids—protohumans or earliest "men"—grew brains that were larger than apes'. In less than two million years—an eyeblink in geologic time—early man's brain size doubled.

As the brain enlarged, so did the head. The larger head could pass through the birth canal only if the female's pelvis were enlarged or if the infant emerged at a low state of development. A pelvis large enough would have made walking (not to mention running with the clan) difficult. If the infant were *too* immature, it could not live outside the womb. So nature compromised. The female pelvis, over the generations, grew broader, and the infants were born well enough developed to survive. But the complex little creature required a long gestation period, plus which its mother needed help during delivery because of its outsized head.

The hominid sire acquired the first traits of fatherhood when he began bringing food to his pregnant mate and stayed around to help her with the birth process. And after prehistoric Dad had helped with the delivery, what did he have? A strange-looking froglet fit for nothing but sucking and crying. Most other babies could walk at birth and follow the pack, but his had months, even years, of growing to do. His mate, as the milk-giver, had to stay put to nurse the infant. Early mamas still used their forearms to help them walk; and as the babies could

"Some males were assigned the task of carrying the eggs."

not cling, they were unable to hit the trail with their males. The father went off to hunt food, which he brought back and shared with *his family*. This is when human sex roles were first foggily defined.

Margaret Mead is among those who feel that this sharing of food is the *sine qua non* of human fatherhood. Man is the only primate who nourishes his family.

Father's social role, especially at the beginning, was a learned one. It had to be taught to the next generation. Teaching required a more complex language, which in turn produced better brains, longer pregnancies, and so forth, until *Homo* became *sapiens*.

The evolution of the father function created the uniquely human style of family structure. The female learned to remain sexually faithful, in return for which she was fed and protected. This saved the male the trouble of snaring a new mate each season. Female humans moved away from the ape's oestrus cycle of fertility and became sexually available and interested throughout their cycles, thus giving the males an added incentive to return home from their hunting expeditions. Social taboos evolved, especially the virtually universal one against mother-son incest. This was enforced by the head of the house. It kept him on the *qui vive*. Over the years, mutuality between a permanent couple may have led to the feeling of affection. The male began to take pride in his function, so that family life brought him rewards independent of survival.

This prehistoric "invention" of the family also marked the differences between a "masculine" and a "feminine" human. Because the males had to be the hunters, it became "masculine" to go out in the world and bring home the bacon. Because the females had to stay with their comparatively helpless young, it became "feminine" to keep the home fires burning.

Patterns of Patriarchy

The social domination of the males, whether a good thing or not, was a natural outgrowth of human genesis. The father, as the stronger parent and protector—physically and later psychologically—wielded the disciplinary fist at home. He trained the offspring to hunt, socializing them as it were.

When society progressed from a life-style based on hunting and gathering to the stage of primitive farming, women tended the garden. Men simply supplemented the diet with meat. In some such societies, women came to have great power. When the people realized that the earth could be made to produce food, and that it was the women who cultivated it, they worshiped female deities, goddesses of the earth and fertility.

Autocrat of the breakfast table

As civilization developed, however, sex roles became routinized and bureaucratized, in sociologist Max Weber's terms. They became habit, custom, tradition. Long after the need for hunting and protection was past, the male continued to play the "strong man." And as economies grew more complex, man went into the marketplace, instead of the forest, and remained the principal provider. By his daily absence from home, a man gained charisma and enhanced his function as a link to society.

Our practical need for fathers, inherited from our post-ape days, was reinforced by the culture, civilization, and religion that our enlarged brains had devised. The chief gods of the Greeks, Romans, Vikings, and most other early Western cultures were male. In the Judeo-Christian tradition we worship a "God the Father." The Old Testament figures were patriarchs, and the early Christians were "Fathers of the Church."

Over the eons, we internalized our need for a father. He was no longer a food-fetcher and physical protector, but he became our value-giver, superego, and emotional backbone. His role was ritualized into patriarchy. He became the god at home, the autocrat of the breakfast table. It was his name that his wife and children took, his word that was law in the family.

Man, in sociologist Talcott Parson's terms, is the "instrumental" sex. He is the tool-user. It would seem natural to a Freudian that male dominance should correlate with the use of tools such as the plow, because of the sexual connotations that "plow" carries with it. A man does, after all, have a tool on his own body that a female lacks.

Women, of course, have used tools, from grinding stones to blenders, looms to sewing machines. But since the days when they had to suckle the hominid young and keep the cave fires burning, feminine tools have been domestic. Masculine tools, whether a stone or a computer program, have been those of the larger society.

Be all that as it may, patriarchal patterns developed from the time early man first used tools. They served to focus his social role and became a father's emblem in the family. Father was the one to teach his children how to

52

use the literal and figurative tools of society. He was the one depended upon for the well-being of his family.

From his physical strength and his practical usefulness, he developed political and social strength. This allowed his family to look up to him and count on him. From the early days of our culture, we have come to assume that children need the toughness and strength symbolized by men as a complement to the softness and warmth that women-the-nurturers have represented.

But quickly, lest the feminists burn this book, it must be said that human society does not *have* to be structured this way. Take matriarchies, for instance.

My Uncle, the Father

Anthropologists would say you'd have a hard time "taking matriarchies," because, they insist, no such thing exists. A "matriarchy," in the social-science definition, is a society in which economic, cultural, and political power is *formally* in the hands of women. By this definition, there are no matriarchies. But there are matri*lineal* cultures, which trace ancestry and property through women. And there are matri*local* ones, in which a husband moves into the wife's home, rather than vice versa.

Some societies combine matriliny and matrilocality, and it is these that come closest to female domination.

The Hopi Indians of the American Southwest are viewed by some anthropologists as among the most extreme examples of female domination. They are a matrilineal and matrilocal society. Women own all property, and the husband is, in effect, a guest who lives on sufferance in his wife's home.

Although he has only minor status in his wife's family, a Hopi father traditionally has considerable influence in his sister's household. This system is called an avunculate. Name and property may pass through the woman's line, but power in the family rests with a woman's brothers, her mother's brothers, and her mother's mother's brothers. All these uncles play what we would call the father's role in providing for the family and socializing the children.

The people of the Trobriand Islands, in the Solomon

Sea off New Guinea, don't even recognize the existence of fathers. According to the anthropologists, the Trobrianders don't make a connection between sex and babies. (Or at least they hadn't figured it out when Polish anthropologist Bronislaw Malinowski studied them in the 1920's.) Intercourse, the Trobrianders maintain, is necessary to open the vagina for the entrance of a spirit sent by the *women's* clan. A married couple lives in the home of the husband's mother's brother, and it is this maternal uncle who exerts discipline and authority over the children and who controls their socialization.

The Trobriand word for "father" means "my mother's husband." He plays the role of babysitter and companion for the child. He fondles and entertains it, but has no special power over it.

The people of the Trobriand Islands may not believe in fathers, but they do provide for *fathering*. In American society, Dad is supposed to combine the Trobriand uncle's discipline with the mother's husband's fondling.

Of course, many fathers in the United States are not "American dads." Among first-, second-, and even third-generation immigrant groups, fathers still may follow patterns established in their countries of origin. In Asian and European civilizations more deeply rooted than the American, fathers tend to be more authoritarian, more distant, and regarded with greater awe than modern American dads. An Italian-American father may still hold absolute dominion over his wife and children—and his children's spouses and children—even when the family is otherwise "Americanized." A German-American father may raise his children with the same strict authority exerted by his German counterparts. A Chinese-American community may still center around a traditional patriarchal hierarchy. In such segments of the rich ethnic mix that makes up America, "What's a father for?" may be a needless question: his role is clearly defined even in the new country.

But in some immigrant families, the father's role may quickly deteriorate—by force of the migration itself. Sociologist Kingsley Davis is among those who point out that social change—and migration is a major social change—can unravel family structure. Hindered by language difficulties and inexperience with new social customs, a newly arrived father may have trouble finding respectable work or exerting authority over his family. To his children, a foreign-born father may represent the old ways that they need to cast off in order to conform to their new peer groups. Old-world fathering habits may succumb to the "strong antiauthoritarian pressures" of American culture, as sociologist Leonard Benson notes.

And are we native Americans *sure* what a father is for? In traditional human societies—or in the animal world—the role the father plays is almost unalterably established by culture or by instincts. In our contemporary society, however, the function of—even the need for—fathers has become a matter for debate. In the midst of such confusion, it is vital to remember that fathers, no matter what their styles of life, do make an invaluable contribution to their children's development.

4

A Man Around
the House

"A father's role in the family? He's just . . . *there.*" Salesman Bert Howard was embarrassed that after three kids and 22 years of being a father, he had no clearer view of his family function. But in a way, his comment sums it up. A father is for being "there." By being a man around the house you probably carry out more fatherly duties than you realize.

Bert Howard knows he's "there." *You* know you're there. But to most "experts" the American father is "almost invisible," as sociologist Leonard Benson puts it. Most students of the American family are not too clear as to what a father does for his children, but they do know what happens when he is *not* there.

Various studies indicate that children with absent fathers have greater difficulty in coping with themselves and with life in general than children whose fathers are present and involved. They tend to be socially irresponsible, to demand immediate gratification for their wants (an index of future failure), to have trouble dealing early with their playmates and later with the opposite sex, and to become too dependent on the values of their peer groups.

A lot of ifs, buts, and maybes are built into that research. Still, one thing is clear: your children *need* you to be there—in body and in spirit.

A functioning father gives to his children stability, strength, self-discipline, guidance, a system of values, appropriate sex-role behavior, and the desire for achievement.

"Me? I'm supposed to do all that?" Accountant Fred Casper was bewildered and alarmed. "All I do is hang around and help out every now and then—I must be a lousy father!" He isn't a lousy father. He's a good one to his two kids, and he is performing all those functions without being aware of it. You probably are, too. How?

Most of your contributions stem from, or are inextricably bound up with, the typical father's central role—that of provider.

Are You Providing More Than a Roof?

"Making good money and getting a good job. Feeding your family, paying the bills. . . . Going to work every morning, coming home with a headache," Lawrence Fuchs (in *Family Matters*) quotes an 11-year-old girl on what it means to be a father. As if you didn't know it, sociologists report that girls and women expect their men to be their providers. Bringing home the bacon—providing the wherewithal to feed, house, and clothe a wife and children—is the role a boy is traditionally trained for. When he contemplates marriage, a young man may have a little idea of what it will be like, and he may have some small awareness of what will be expected of him as a parent. But what he probably knows for sure is that he will have to be the main breadwinner of the ménage.

Employers find that family men make the most reliable and productive workers. This may simply be because they are fed more regularly than bachelors, but *you* know that it's also because a father has people who count on him getting that paycheck and having it increased every now and then.

Divorced fathers are still expected to support their children. Our traditional view of father-as-provider is so entrenched that after divorce a father may be required to contribute support even though his ex-wife has greater resources than he does.

Life-styles are changing. More women are working. But few men have yet trained themselves to be anything *but* workers. As a result, your job probably means a lot to you personally. If you are like most men, you tend to identify with the work you do. For many fathers, the job may become the focus of life, no matter how important they say their families are. Men in our culture who are unable to fulfill the provider role, whether through disability or social inequity, endure severe blows to their egos.

Bert Howard's main regret, looking back over his life as a father, is that he wasn't able to be a "better" provider, even though his kids were adequately fed, clothed, and educated. Knowing that you insure the good life for your family does bring satisfaction apart from the job itself.

Your job may also be the key to your status at home, and outside it. It determines the amount of clout you wield. Studies of power within the family show that influence over decisions parallels income distribution. If a father is the only breadwinner in the family, his authority is likely to be less often challenged than if other members make financial contributions.

The type of work a man does and the salary he earns affect his standing in the community and his image in the eyes of his wife and children. Family and friends tend to regard an architect more highly than a hod carrier, and a *successful* architect is more admired and respected than one who is a failure.

Providing for his family is so essential that a father may wrap himself too tightly in the role. Chain-store executive Carl Bartlett, for instance, worked long hours, took almost weekly business trips, and frequently moved his family around in an effort to increase his earnings. He was so bent on being a "good provider" that, although he said he was on the job "for the family," he rarely *saw* his wife and three kids.

Some men come to resent their wife and children for "trapping" them into a routine that tires and bores them for much of their lives. Or a man may get so hung up on his importance as a provider and on the power that goes with it, that he expects to be treated with royal respect when he is at home. He becomes instead a royal pain, alienating the very mate and offspring he is caring for.

Why has society placed the providing burden so squarely on the shoulders of the male? As we saw in the previous chapter, the tradition developed long before civilization did. The fact that most Americans continue to follow this prehistoric pattern does not mean that providing need only be a *male* role. Indeed, many abuses have been committed against women in the name of traditional masculine "superiority." Men are not superior. They are different from women in ways that have made them the customary providers.

"Society is the way it is because people are the way they are," comments Louise Bates Ames of the Gesell Institute of Child Development, "and it's unlikely that masculine and feminine roles are going to change." If they are, it is going to happen slowly. Despite a new spirit among women in various parts of the country, the traditional sex-linked social functions haven't been reversed.

It takes only a glance at the crowds on commuter trains, the people driving in rush-hour traffic, or the workers leaving a factory at quitting time to learn who is still the chief provider. It's you, Dad.

Bringing Home the Bacon—Plus

As the family member who is the one most likely to be working away from home, or dealing with nonrelated people from a home-based office, shop, or farm, the father is the family's link with that world beyond itself. He becomes a "surrogate for society."

"Frankly, I can't say that I feel, when I put my key in the door at night, that I'm opening up some gateway from the outside world," social worker Ray Kantor admits. Few fathers do. But whether you realize it or not, when you lug that hard-earned bacon home, you bring with it the ideas, values, demands, and customs from the society on the other side of the front door.

Fred Casper came home one night to find his 4-year-old daughter pummeling her little sister. "Ellie! Stop that!" he ordered.

"But she keeps touching my picture!"

"That doesn't mean you can hit her. Did you *ask* her not to touch it?"

"No."

"Well, next time, ask before you get angry."

Ellie's father has conveyed the message that, in our society, we at least *try* to settle differences with words before resorting to force. Her mother can and does invoke the same rules. But this and all the other spoken and unspoken lessons have greater standing and more lasting effect because they come from the parent who seems to keep in closer contact with the mysterious world where such rules are made.

Reading his paper, John Green starts swearing over the day's disclosures of political corruption. His 7-year-old son asks what's the matter.

"The people who are running our government lie, and cheat, and break the law—*that's* what's the matter!"

"She keeps touching my picture."

60

"What's going to happen to them, Dad?"

"Well, I think we've caught them. Now that people have found out about it, we're not going to let them get away with it."

John Green's son learns that lying, cheating, and law-breaking anger his father. And he picks up the notion that a citizen must be concerned about the government he lives under. All that from the man who brought the paper home from downtown.

"Go reason with your daughter," shoe-store manager Jack Rose's wife told him as he walked in the door from work. "She wants to quit school and get a job."

"Look, I see these young girls working downtown," Jack tells his 16-year-old. "Their jobs aren't worth peanuts. They're boring and low-paid, and they don't lead anywhere. Which would you rather do, suffer through one more year of school, or be a waitress the rest of your life? Believe me, it isn't so glamorous."

Not only does Jack's daughter get information on the job outlook from a man on the scene, but she can think about the fact that, in order to cope with the larger society, it may be better to put off an immediate satisfaction for future fulfillment. She also gains the idea that her father thinks that she's a self worth disciplining.

"Daddy, are you a scientist?"

"No, Tim, I'm a computer programmer."

"What's *that*?"

As Frank Stevens tries to explain to his son what his job is and how it fits into the broad scope of the working world, Tim learns something about technology, society, and the economy—and this has a special meaning for him, because his Dad is part of it.

Interchanges like these are probably part of the daily routine at your house, too. Contact and conversation with the parent who arrives from a job "out there somewhere" amid a flurry of excited greetings—that's all "value-giving" and "socialization" are.

As dentist Henry Ross shrewdly points out, "I think I

give my kids their values or whatever just by being myself. Not that I'm perfect, but I'm satisfied, and nothing I can tell them will mean anything if I don't act it out."

A father who preaches honesty to his kids but boasts of his own sharp practices, or one who, in an alcoholic haze, calls on his children to "master themselves so they can master the world," is simply not going to have a positive effect. Your children will take on your values, and through you those of the society at large, more from what you do than from what you say.

They will sense, from the way you look when you come in that door, whether you like your job or the world you have just left. The moods you bring home, as well as the kind of work you do, can set the whole tone for your household life.

Your opinion, expressed by word or by posture, is terribly important to your children. They will learn, by the way you shrug off your day, or laugh about it, or snarl at it, whether work and society are useful tools, necessary nuisances, or evils to be avoided.

Your regular return home, your patience in bearing up under whatever happened before you got there, come to stand for protection and stability in your children's minds. They reinforce the feelings your size and strength have given them from earliest infancy.

The ideal father—like the ideal society—stands for competence, responsibility, self-discipline, compassion, and justice. He is the kind of man a child will strive to please.

Great Expectations?

Your good opinion of them is dear to your children. To gain it, they will exert great efforts to meet the standards you set for them. It is by setting reasonable standards that we make our children want to grow. High expectations, within limits, compliment and encourage a child. "My Dad thinks I can do that—well, I guess I can at least try."

It tends to fall to you, Dad, to set up these expectations. For one thing, you know best what the outside world demands for success. But it also may be a *male* role. Good mothering is vital, for without mother's early nurturing, children will never feel good about themselves. But a mother's relationship with her children calls for her to accept them as they *are*, so she may be less able than you are to guide them toward what they *can* be. She may view the kids as her babies. Her body produced them. A father's part in the creative process is to make people out of those babies—people with values, personalities, and goals.

On the other hand, their mother probably does know your children more intimately than you do. If she deals with them every day, all day, and encounters their successes and failures when they occur, she may have a better idea than you about what demands are reasonable for an individual child.

From the pediatrician, from child-care books she has read (which most fathers don't), and from her observations of neighbors' children, she gets a sense of the developmental patterns all children share. Fathers who don't understand these patterns, or who have some ideal child in mind rather than their real one, may try to impose the wrong standards *at the wrong time*.

"No son of mine is going to wet his pants," the father of a 2-year-old thunders. So the kid keeps peeing inappropriately, only now he worries about why he's unable to do what this tall father-god thinks is right.

"No child of mine is going to lie!" another father roars, not realizing that to a 4-year-old lying isn't dishonesty as adults know it, but a kind of wish fulfillment through fantasy.

Being able to keep dry pants and to tell the truth are of course good goals for any child. But a father who raises such expectations at an inappropriate time will only see his hopes dashed. Over a period of time he will lose his credibility as a standard-setter. Worse, a child who sees himself as continually failing to come up to his father's expectations will begin to feel that there is something wrong with him.

Radio engineer Harry Irving's son was a bookworm, but his father thought he should be an athlete. "I didn't realize how he was suffering under the pressure I was putting on him till he began doing badly in school. He'd always been a good student, but when he found out he wasn't as good as I thought he could be at sports, I guess he sort of gave up on everything."

A father cannot overestimate the importance he has in the life of his child. To a baby, the big one with the deep voice is thrilling because he isn't Mommy. A toddler who doesn't seem to be listening can repeat word for word everything that Daddy said. An older child will invoke his father as a protector—"My Dad can beat up your Dad"—or an authority—"My Dad says. . . ."

Your children want to please you. They want to match your expectations of them if they possibly can. Once a father has won the trust of his children and justified their respect in him, the best standard he can set is: "I know that you'll do the best you can." That's demanding, but flexible. It implies that you believe that there is a "best" they can do.

Fostering a feeling of self-worth is one of a father's most important jobs. From a child's point of view, Mommy says "good girl" because she "has to"—of course Mommy loves her and is pleased. But when Daddy says "good girl," it's because he really means it and is proud. "When children feel important to fathers," writes Dr. O. Spurgeon English, "they feel important to others." Discipline, compassion, striving, creativity—all the best human characteristics flow from the concept, "I am worthwhile, so I can produce something of value."

"I want my kids to know what they want and to have the self-confidence to get it," is the way lawyer Chris Scholl put it. Bert Howard, ghetto-born Tom Victor, and other fathers agree that this kind of goal is the best to set for their children.

How do these fathers expect to give their children such self-confidence? "Make them feel loved and important." "*Listen* to them." "Try not to overwhelm them, but stand back and let them see what *they* can do."

Values Are Worth It

"If he can understand and value himself," Ray Kantor says of his son, "he will do the same for others." That's the kind of ideal that many of the fathers I spoke with hope to instill in their children. For too many people, the modern world seems a valueless place, where the future is at best uncertain. When George Forrest was growing up, he says, "I thought of happiness in terms of having a good profession, being rich and successful. But now I'm pessimistic about the way the world is and will be in the future. It's hard to know whether there will be such a thing as happiness when my kids are grown—or how to help them achieve it."

Today's generations of parents grew up either during a war or in an era of "peacetime" air-raid drills. We convinced ourselves, with the help of our frightened elders, that the atomic bomb was sure to wipe us out, if not this week, then next. Today, we are eating ourselves alive, destroying our environment and our natural resources at an indigestible rate.

"What is the point of values in a doomed world?" some parents wonder. Or, "What values can I give today, when tomorrow is going to be so different?" Social traditions are crumbling. Sexual standards seem to shift with the introduction of each new contraceptive. The word "honesty" provokes laughter. We rely on violence to protect ourselves from violence.

Father may be the value-giver, but what values can he give?

"To not hurt himself, and to not hurt anyone else." "To be at peace with himself." "To be honest with himself." "To respect himself, so that he can respect others." "To share—everything with everybody." The fathers I've talked with who hold out such standards are saying to their kids neither "Do your own thing," nor "My way is the right way." They are saying, "You have a best—be it, and find it in everyone else." This is not the same as "Be the best, and beat out the rest." If you can instill such ideals, you can create in your children a desire, if not to reform the world, then at least to make the best of their own corner of it.

Turning the TV Off—on Yourself

Okay, so there are values to transmit. But how? "By being the way you *are*," says Bert Howard. Children learn to "be" by what psychology calls "identification." Child psychoanalyst Selma Fraiberg calls identification a "two-way process."

"A child," she writes, "acquires the capacity to extend himself beyond the boundaries of his own ego, to occupy imaginatively the egos of other human beings and hence 'to know how others feel'. . . . But he also has the capacity to take other egos into his, to incorporate . . . certain aspects of the personality of another person, to make certain qualities of that personality his own. In the case of moral development, the judgments, standards, values of beloved persons are taken over by the child, made part of his own personality."

Children identify with their mothers as well as their fathers, of course. But it is identification with Daddy, stronger, louder, more forceful, coming in from that strange outer world, that can build a strong moral confidence.

No child can identify with a man who breezes in the door and settles down with his beer and peanuts in front of the TV for the evening. "Sure, I spend five, six hours a day with my kids," I've heard fathers boast. What most of them mean is that they're watching television and they don't make a fuss if the kids watch it too.

Larry Downs ran a small tool-making business he'd inherited from his father. He didn't love the work above all else, but it was reasonably satisfying and earned him

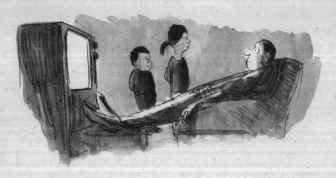

If you flop in front of the TV, you flop as a father.

and his family a good living. Every night he'd come home, eat dinner, and watch TV in his bedroom till he fell asleep during the late show. He couldn't understand why his son didn't want to come into the business, or why the young man had such trouble getting along with girls. He never did figure out why his daughter married a slob or why she couldn't achieve anything she set out to do. If he had turned the TV off sometimes, things might have been different.

Television is terrific. I'm an addict. It brings the universe to our living room and vice versa. It can stimulate the mind and imagination, and offer escape to anywhere and nowhere from an easy chair. It can also make us yearn for things we don't need and lead us to value ideas that are really only stage sets.

Worse, it takes you away from your family. When my husband watches television, which is thankfully rare, his eyes glaze over and he becomes unreachable. In fact, he has even been known to express annoyance when his wife or child succeeds in breaking his concentration!

If you flop in front of the TV all evening every evening, you can flop as a father. It is not only because your kids can't make contact with you and what you should represent. They learn that *you* value television. So they get their values from the box.

This is not to say that television cannot be used as an effective means to bring families together. It can be a medium for transmitting the messages you want to share with your children. Because a father was willing, for instance, to answer questions during news broadcasts, more than a few children have gained sophisticated insights into what happens in the world, and what Daddy thinks about it. But viewed constantly with a "Shut-up-I'm-busy" attitude, it can prevent the development of the relationship you need with your children if they are to incorporate the best of your identity.

When Your Boy Wants a Doll

Of course, it may just be that a father uses the TV (or overtime, or golf) as an escape from a role he doesn't understand or feel confident about.

Success is the keynote of the American man's life. He is pressured to do things well, and if he doesn't understand how to do something, he'd rather not try. Since boys are not trained to be fathers, it's little wonder that as men they shy away from a game whose rules they don't know.

"Men are characteristically less patient with children or with immaturity and incompetence of any kind, unless that is precisely what they have been trained for," sociologist Leonard Benson writes. "Then, as in related areas of work that are routinely identified as feminine, men characteristically develop the skill to an even higher level than women." Such male chauvinism aside, I have been interested to find that many of the fathers who are most intimately involved in the day-to-day affairs of their children are the ones who have had some sort of experience with children before becoming fathers. Either they have cared for very young siblings, nieces, or nephews while they were growing up, or they have some kind of training related to child development—psychology, medicine, teaching, and the like.

A man who hasn't seen a diaper since the last time he wore one is less likely to change his new baby's pants than a man who has some more ongoing experience with others' bodily functions or with the stages of human development.

It is more than an understandable dislike of diapers. It is a feeling that there is some spiritual connection between a female and her offspring that leads men to turn their children over exclusively to women for raising.

To be good fathers, men may have to learn how, and people are beginning to teach them. Under a program designed by the Department of Health, Education, and Welfare, a number of high schools across the country have instituted "parenthood education" classes. Boys and girls can learn, through practice and discussion, about children and about their own future roles as parents. In 1973 the University of Akron, in Akron, Ohio, introduced a course in fatherhood that has been extremely well attended. Even out of school and into parenthood, fathers are learning more about their role through courses in "Parent Effectiveness Training," available in various parts of the country. If you haven't the time or inclination for formal schooling in fatherhood, a look through some of the books listed in the appendix might give you the confidence and the motivation to tear yourself away from television.

William's Doll, a children's story by Charlotte Zolotow, is about a little boy who asked to have a doll. His father panicked and presented him with a baseball mitt, a badminton set, and other "masculine" toys, all of which the little boy appreciated. But he still wanted a doll. His grandmother understood. She explained that William wanted a doll so he could learn how to be a *father*.

Were your son to ask for a doll, would you turn livid? Would you hide in front of the TV and let your wife "handle it"? Or would you be able to take it as a compliment that your son thought enough of fathers to want to practice to be as good a one as you are?

Stamping Down

William's father put his foot down about the doll. Was that discipline? No. That was only the irrational exertion of power. Fathers have traditionally been the "disciplinarians"—the court of last resort, the ultimate threat. Discipline is not a synonym for "punishment." Discipline means "teaching."

It was once thought that a child learned to control his behavior out of *fear* of the wrath of his father or God. But the only effective long-term discipline is *self*-discipline, and current expertise rightly holds that fear is the least effective motivation for self-discipline. A child who refrains from an action because he fears his father's punishment is not disciplining himself, but relying on his parent for appropriate punishment after he does the deed. A child learns to govern himself when a warm relationship with his parents makes him *want* to follow their rules and live up to their expectations.

Does this mean that a father cannot actively discipline his children, or mete out the punishment that is a part of discipline? No. As Georgetown University psychologists Juan Cortes and Florence Gatti note, "children must learn to accept restraints on their behavior, and it is the father who is most likely to impose these restraints."

Many older fathers I've talked with, who raised kids during the era when "permissiveness" was in vogue, regret that they didn't impose tighter restraints on their children. The younger ones are setting narrower limits for their kids than they lived with themselves. John Green explains, "My folks were great, but sometimes I had too *few* rules, and I felt lost."

Author Lawrence Fuchs, urging the "restoration of the father," cites children's need for authority, which he calls "the *legitimized* exercise of power in the performance of responsibility." Your legitimate exercise of power may have more effect than your wife's because of your louder voice, your greater size, your longer absences from home, or your tighter control of the purse. But that doesn't mean that "discipline" in your household should rely on your wife's threats of "wait till your father gets home." Not only does such delayed justice have little impact, but it casts you in the role of an ogre.

Stepping In

Some things do have to wait till you get home. You have a special perspective if you are away all day. A working father has a distance from his children and their problems that an at-home mother lacks. You can use this distance creatively by training a fresh eye on a knotty situation. This may warrant your stepping in to resolve the conflict. Your wife will have this same perspective if she goes to work. Be careful—don't step on each other's toes in your efforts to "step in." It could be agreed on between you beforehand as to who solves what problems in which areas.

Ray Kantor, from his viewpoint as a caseworker in a clinic for disturbed children, feels that "stepping in" is a vital function of fatherhood. "I work with some severely troubled kids who wouldn't be there if the father hadn't seen problems the mother wouldn't admit," he says. "But more often, I see serious problems of behavior and development that could have been prevented *if* the father had not maintained the attitude that the kids were his wife's responsibility. A man who is out of the house can spot trouble if he looks for it, and should step in to head it off."

Fathers—and working mothers—too often are attacked on all flanks with the day's problems as soon as they walk through the door. It is tempting to retreat. Don't. And if there are two of you, you can divide and diffuse the children's assaults. Stepping in is an important role. It takes tact, too. If your wife *has* been with the kids all day, and if you ride in on a high horse and ask her why she's doing what she's doing in the obviously wrong way she's doing it, you are likely to get a well-deserved clap in the teeth. But you can, and should, wait for a restful moment and talk quietly with her or your kids about whatever concerns you. It may be a report card, or a fight that seems to have been raging since you left home. You may sense an atmosphere of tension, or notice that a child's room is inordinately neat or surprisingly messy. Take the time to feel out your home, to wonder, and to ask.

"Wait till your father gets home!"

Your wife may need you to "step in" with some extra muscle for household chores or energy for entertaining the kids. She needs your moral support as well. Giving her a hand helps give her some of the strength and satisfaction she needs to be the kind of mother you want for your children. And it strengthens your marriage, too.

Some men have frankly told me that they could do without their wives, but they count on a close relationship with their kids. Like it or not, you need your wife! She can make or break your influence over the children. As Louise Ames of the Gesell Institute points out, a mother can say at the dinner table, "You see, I told you your father would say that," and communicate, simply by the tilt of an eyebrow or the tone of her voice, either a positive or a negative view of you.

Do you suppose your wife says, "I wish your father would get here soon," or "Why is your father always late!"? Would she advise, "You can ask Daddy to fix it—I know he'd want to try, but he may be very tired tonight," or, "You can *ask* your father to fix it, but he'll probably *say* he's too tired." It all depends on how she feels about you.

Is Sex a Battle?

For your own sanity, as you must know by now, you need to get along well with your wife. A happy relationship with your wife is an important influence on your children, too. Policeman Dick Fogarty is right when he says, "I think loving my wife is about the best thing I can do for my kids." As some of those uh-huh studies have demonstrated, happy marriages make happy children, who in turn make happy marriages. In the course of his social work, Ray Kantor has noticed that the parents of many disturbed children are themselves emotionally troubled as a result of their own pathological parenting.

Children whose parents are working together toward the same goal, whether it's recycling the trash or building a business; or who are supporting each other in separate endeavors; or are amicably working out disagreements gain a good understanding of how people can cooperate. For those children, future sex, like life, needn't become a battle.

72

5

Are You Sorry You Had a Girl?

Are you sorry you had a girl? Nowadays, the fashionable response—perhaps the only safe one—is, "Of course not." That's what Jerry Carl, the father of a young son and daughter, said when I asked *him*. He's a with-it guy, definitely turned into today's style of life and thought. Hardly anyone would call him a male chauvinist. And he obviously *loves* his daughter a lot. But he answered all my questions as though he had only a son: "What I hope for *him*...," "The biggest problem *he* has given me...," "I want to give *him* a feeling of *his* own worth."

When Jerry's wife pointed out that he was speaking as though his daughter didn't exist, he was stunned. "Me? Are you sure? Well, I'll be damned!"

Sexism may lurk in even the most liberated among us.

Society may have conditioned men like Jerry to ignore daughters despite themselves. Or fathers may stand back from their daughters because they don't know how to relate to them. Or it simply may be that they feel they have little to offer a girl.

The opposite is true.

"Father's role seems to be of great significance in the process of feminine identification and personal adjustment in the female," psychologist Henry Biller writes. A study sponsored by the National Institute of Mental Health found that father absence was harder on girls without siblings than on single boys. And social researcher Mary M. Thomas reports that, in the group she studied, father absence had a greater overall adverse effect on girls than on boys.

As your little girl gets bigger, you as a father stand as an example from which she learns how to relate to men. From your responses to her and your expectations of her, she will form her own definition of womanhood.

Some of her sex-role behavior she will learn by your approval or disapproval. Some, she will learn by observing how you deal with women. And some she will learn by actually practicing on you.

Electra Did Her Mother In

Laura is 4 years old. She could do without her mother, except maybe at mealtimes. She thinks her Daddy is terrific. She plants big wet kisses on his cheek when he walks in from work (and wipes her mother's kisses off). She likes to snuggle in bed with Daddy, and makes mudsuppers for him. She wants to marry Daddy when she grows up.

Laura is in the throes of a female version of the Oedipus complex. Psychiatrists label this phase "Electra," on the basis of an ancient Greek myth. Electra, the story goes, was furious with her mother, Clytemnestra, for having Agamemnon, her father, killed to protect an extramarital affair. She goaded her brother, Orestes, into killing their mother.

Now, it isn't necessary for your wife to have an affair and plot your demise for your daughter to be angrily jealous of her. The little girl, the theory goes, just wants to win you away from her. Hopefully, your little "Electra" won't knock her mother off in order to gain your exclusive favors (though she may have guilt-ridden fantasies and nightmares about doing just that). She *is* going to try to win you. She *has* to try, if she is to develop a healthy sexual identity. She doesn't know about marriage vows or fidelity, but she does know that there is something wrong with trying to take Mommy's place. The harder she tries, in her little-girl way, to seduce the most important man in her life, the guiltier she may feel about cutting in on Mommy, and the more clearly she will realize that she has a long way to grow before becoming enough of a woman for you.

It is important that you show her that you find her charming, that you are flattered by her attentions (and most fathers *are*), but you politely and firmly turn down her advances. If the occasion arises, when she proposes, for instance, you might explain to her that you are married to Mommy, but that you're glad she wants to "marry" a man like you. When she grows up, you hope that she will find a man *like* you to love. With such assurance, she's on her way toward appropriate sex-role behavior. What she will do is learn to be "like Mommy," the woman who did manage to win your affections.

Every father's daughter goes through this stage, some

She will try to seduce you in her little girl way.

more obviously than others, and they all need their father's wise cooperation. If you maintain too wide a distance, or reject her childish propositions too harshly, some psychoanalysts counsel, your daughter may either idealize you and thus form an unrealistic concept of men, or she will be unable and unwilling to give love to men at all.

Freud believed that a little girl's strivings were tied to a "castration fear." Having noticed that she had no penis, she thought, according to this theory, that it had been cut off and that she could get it back by pleasing her father, the one in the family who was sure to have one. Penis envy is a very male-oriented idea, and more recent theories surmise that the girl is simply trying the feminine role on for size when she goes after her dad. Still, it does seem to help a little girl's self-image to explain that she was born with a vagina and a uterus in which babies can grow when she's bigger, rather than letting her worry about having "no penis."

Whatever the source of the "Electra complex," your daughter will take it under cover from about the age 6 until early adolescence. During these "middle years," she will concentrate on imitating her mother and on exploring her own humanness.

When your daughter becomes a teen-ager, however, Electra may come out of hiding. She will try to provoke you—sexually (in a veiled way), and obnoxiously. She will demand your attention as her father and as a man.

At 14, Sally liked to sit on her father's lap while they were watching TV. She always managed to break up her parents' cozy conversations. She would get into furious fights with her mother during which she would try to get her father to side with her. She would "forget" to close her door when she was dressing. She loved going places with her father, even to baseball games, though she hated baseball. When she started dating, she would bring home strange specimens of male adolescence, as if to say, "Rescue me," or "Fight for me."

That's exactly what she *was* saying, subconsciously. As she became aware of her sexuality, she wanted to try out her new feelings on the safest and most beloved man she knew, her father. Any father would be flattered by such attentions from a sweet young thing, and some fathers might be worried about triggering the sexual time bomb their daughters had turned into. A father needs to show, by word and deed, that he is happy his daughter has discovered heterosexuality and that he understands her feelings, but that some behavior is inappropriate.

He also needs to be her knight in shining armor, by protecting her with reasonable rules and limitations. In that way, even if she can't try her sex out on him directly, at least she knows that he is watching over her while she begins to explore the world of other men.

As your daughter grows out of adolescence, if you and she have successfully managed this often unconscious "affair," she will go on to be the kind of woman that you hope she will be. The men that she becomes involved with or marries will be startlingly like yourself. They will be ones whom you will eventually (all fathers who love their daughters feel a certain amount of jealousy toward their "competitors" at first) come to respect.

We have talked about a father's "wise cooperation" in his daughter's sexual development. Does this mean that the male in you will somehow magically feel no physical attraction for your budding woman? No. The literature on pathological families indicates that more fathers than you might imagine do successfully lust after their daughters. Predictably, such experiences distort a girl's sexual identification, not to mention the family problems they can cause.

Father-daughter incest is not a good idea. If you're tempted—get help. There's something wrong. But a lot of fathers reveal (and few books discuss) a definite, but controlled, attraction for their daughters. "I think Helen has a lovely bottom," Ray Kantor says of his toddling daughter. "I'm proud of the broad shoulders and tapering hips Josh has—even envious. But I can think of Helen as a girl. I can see her mother in her, and, yes, I think she's an attractive female. I relate to females that way—if I didn't, after all, neither Josh nor Helen would be here."

Exactly. Old-fashioned fathers might stimulate "femininity" by praising their daughters' "domestic ability," by comparing them favorably with their mothers, and by complimenting them on their appearance, as all the handbooks used to advise. But they also have affirmed their daughters' sexuality by a certain attitude, a certain look that says, "You are a damned good-looking girl."

Before the shrinks accuse me of advocating intrafamilial orgies, let me emphasize that this doesn't mean that you *tell* your daughter she has a lovely bottom, or pinch it. You don't help her get dressed or allow her to take showers with you at all ages. You don't return her little-girl pecks with grown-up kisses. It just means that a certain amount of cross-sexual attraction is common within families, and, when controlled, probably normal. A father who feels so guilty about such feelings that he represses them completely may give his daughter the impression that she is *not* attractive to men.

It's important to be aware of the contributions you make to your daughter's sexual identification, even though most of them will be automatic and unconscious. You don't turn your little girl into a woman by moral precept or even by calculated example. Vital to her self-concept is simply the feeling that you are happy she's a girl. If she senses that, then she will be happy, too, and with your help she can work out her idea of girlness. If she doesn't, she will never be sure who she is.

With short hair, strong muscles, tanned leathery skin, Henrietta Braun looked like a man. Long before it was fashionable, she dressed like a man. When she did put on a dress, it was ratty and patched, announcing her feeling that she was ashamed to be a woman.

"My father wanted a boy," she explained. "He was terribly disappointed when I came out female, and he gave me the name he'd pick for his son—Henry, only feminized."

Around the office where we both worked, everyone called her Henry. We made jokes about her, I'm afraid, but we pitied her and were bewildered by her. She wasn't homosexual, she wasn't heterosexual, she wasn't anything but lonely. She couldn't relate to men, and she couldn't get close to women. She was bright and competent, but the manner and appearance she had adopted to please her long-dead father kept her from achieving much of anything. She was an unhappy person all her life simply because her father had been sorry that she was born female and had raised her to be a man.

Having a close relationship with your daughter, having her "identify" with you, does not mean that she will grow into a lesbian or a "masculine" woman. Research shows instead that a satisfying relationship with a father is necessary if a little girl is to grow into a real woman.

What Is a Woman's Place?

You know by now, unless you're further out of it than Rip Van Winkle, that a "real" woman's place is not just in the home. A woman is as capable, strong, creative, and intelligent as the next person. Just the feeling that a statement like that has to be written makes some modern women justifiably angry. Men shouldn't have to be told that women are equal. And most fathers today probably *don't* have to be told. But unless your consciousness has been adequately raised, you may unknowingly be squeezing your daughter into some pigeonhole marked "just a girl."

As your little girl grows up, it is her mother she is imitating, but it is you she is trying to please. The type of woman you married will influence the type of daughter you raise. If you like to see a woman tied to the stove, and if your daughter likes you, she'll tie herself there. "I've noticed that boys and girls are different," Art Robbins, a young doctor, admits. "And yes, I treat them differently. But I hope any daughter of mine would grow up to be as intelligent and active as my wife is."

Are your signals clear? If you have dreams of your daughter taking over your business, but refuse to allow her mother to do more than help out as a receptionist, it will be hard for her to be a career woman. If you think you are pointing her toward graduate school, but you praise her mother only for her cooking, she's going to be confused about her goals.

From you, your daughter has to learn how to deal with the opposite sex. By living with you, she catalogs the qualities to look for in a man. This means, ideally, that you treat her *and* her mother with affection and respect. But you can go too far, as a lot of fathers still do, in playing the courtly "big daddy."

Dr. Spock says: "Fathers' relationships with their daughters are just as crucial as with their sons. Girls learn how to be women primarily from their mothers. But there's the other half of the human race that girls and women have to learn to get along with and even marry. This they learn first of all from living with and loving their fathers. So fathers have to be suitably livable and lovable. Some fathers, particularly those who are no longer getting along as comfortably with their wives as they used to, become a bit too mushy or cuddly with their daughters. This is not ideal, and may make it more difficult for the daughters to achieve an ideal maturity and independence in adulthood. This is not the kind of lovableness I have in mind. A father should be showing his daughters a parental rather than a romantic affection and a warm appreciation of their capabilities and their individualities."

Father-daughter research in the 1960's discloses that a "masculine" father will produce a "feminine" daughter. But these days, a father who, in overdoing his stereotypically masculine role, overemphasizes his daughter's stereotypically feminine role, is doing her a disservice. She will encounter opportunities and demands in the future that she won't be able to cope with unless you've helped her to be a thinking human as well as a woman.

More than Sugar and Spice

The basic gift a father can give his daughter is a sense of her identity as a human being.

You play a key role in helping your daughter to feel that she *can* be and do anything she wants to. She doesn't have to learn to play baseball, though you shouldn't keep her from it. You needn't ply her with fire engines instead of dolls, though she should have "boys'" toys if she wants them. You don't have to show your disappointment if you've groomed her for a high-powered career and then she "just" gets married.

"Yes, yes," you say, "and what else is new? We all know

about the evils of sexism." And yet, as Jerry Carl demonstrated in his interview, there's many a slip twixt intention and act. Feminists are absolutely right in pointing out that parents channel girls, often unconsciously and by force of habit, into "female interests" and away from those activities which the past reserved for men.

You are a powerful person, Dad, and it doesn't take much to make your daughter stay a "girl" forever. Just in case, check yourself against this list of still-common slip-ups:

• Do you compliment her more for being pretty than for being smart?

• Do you ever read her storybooks that contain lines like, "Isn't that just like a girl to cry"?

• Do you ever shut her out of a current-events debate in which she wants to join?

• Have you ever even wished she'd go off and get married so you could more easily afford college for her brother?

• Do you ever—*ever*—comment, even casually, "Because you're a girl, you can't. . . " (fill in almost any activity besides "grow a beard" or "use the men's room").

Your answers to all of the above, of course, should be a resounding "Never!"

But that's the negative angle on fathering a daughter. Fathers who have produced daughters who could successfully meet any challenge are the ones who always assumed that a girl can do anything, given the necessary self-assurance and encouragement. And you're the one to give her that.

6

Fathering a Man

A boy needs a father to help him become a man. Some say, too, that a father needs a son in order to feel like a man.

The number of sons a man has correlates with his status in many cultures, and ours is no great exception. In the past, a man's transmittal of traditional and practical wisdom to his male children was assumed to be part of the natural order of things. The father-son relationship was ritualized. "From father to son" became a cliché.

A man can still wield power through his sons—or bask in the reflection of their successes. Of the men I've talked with, most are in favor of equalization of the sexes, and all are sensitive to charges of "male chauvinism." Yet the majority are happy they have sons—or wish they had one—or will try for one within the limits of their feasible family size.

Writing on the motivations for fatherhood, psychoanalyst Therese Benedek suggests that sons offer greater gratification to men than daughters because a boy presents a more obvious example to a father of the survival of his own line. Men seem to think it's easier—and more fun—to raise a son than to raise a daughter. "I feel closer to my son because I can see more of myself in him," one father explained. "I don't know how I would raise a girl," another said, "but since I was a boy, I do know what boys need for growth." Fathers enjoy being boys again with their sons, and some who sire only girls miss that pleasure.

It may be hard on some fathers not to have a son, but it is much harder on a boy not to have a father. Studies of boys in father-absent homes differ in their variables and so produce some conflicting results, but most point to the conclusion, as psychologist Henry Biller writes, that "availability of the father is an important factor in the masculine development of young boys." In general, boys separated from their fathers either show more dependent and "feminine" traits and behavior than boys in father-present homes, or they become excessively aggressive in an apparent attempt to compensate for the strong female influence in their lives. Biller points out that "absence" is not necessarily the opposite of "presence." A boy who lives with both parents may suffer from "father-absence" if his father is not *available* for interaction.

A boy needs a father to help him become a man. Raising a son is as simple as that—and as complicated. What does a boy need from his father? And what does it mean to be a "man" today—and tomorrow?

Your son will get one of his first, and most basic, lessons in "how to be a man" quite early in life. He will learn it from you, even if you don't say a word. He will try to seduce your wife.

Oedipus Loved His Mother

Sophocles made a tragedy of the story of Oedipus. Tom Lehrer wrote a comic song about it. Sigmund Freud named a complex after it. Back in ancient Greece, little Oedipus was abandoned by his parents and brought up by shepherds. When he was grown, he killed his father without knowing it was his father. Then he married his mother without knowing who *she* was. When he discovered what he had done, he put out his own eyes. Neat.

Freud found in the Oedipus tale an analogy to what he

believed all little boys experienced on the way to man-hood. Sometime between the ages of 3 and 5, according to the theory, a boy begins to lust after his mother. He has always loved her, but now his love is focused in a passionate way. His father is his competitor, his archrival whom he may wish dead or at least out of the way for a while. He knows that Mommy belongs to Daddy, and that Daddy is considerably bigger than he is. So he fears, Freud theorized, that if he should succeed in making a conquest of Mommy, or if Daddy catches him making his terrible wishes, Daddy will inflict a harsh, but appropriate, punishment—he will castrate him.

Since, at 4, he's not ready to be a eunuch, he gives up his active quest of Mommy and starts imitating his father, the man who *did* win the lady of the house.

Since Freud's time, a number of psychologists have softened his theory of the Oedipus complex, especially the castration part. Just as it is no longer assumed that children are socialized by fear of their father's punishment, so it is thought that a little boy may not give up on his mother from fear of castration. Psychoanalyst Tess

At four, he's not ready to be a eunuch.

Forrest surmises that during the "Oedipal" stage a boy may simply be learning about being a man by imitating his father's role with his mother.

Some writers, among them William Homan in *Child Sense*, maintain that an Oedipus phase is not a necessary part of normal development. Critics of Freud's theory have pointed out that, since Freud thought the Oedipus phase was universal, and it probably is not, he may have been completely wrong about it. But other students of child development, among them child psychoanalyst Selma Fraiberg and Dr. Benjamin Spock, note that something like the Oedipus story does happen in the lives of virtually all small boys. Some show what they are experiencing more clearly than others.

At the age of 3, John Jr. began ignoring John Sr.'s arrival home. He avoided Daddy's kisses. He wanted to go everywhere with his mother, and lost interest in all the activities he had recently enjoyed with his father. He kept asking when Daddy was going on a trip. He displayed an uncanny ability to interrupt his parents' most passionate moments, and he suddenly developed nighttime needs that had the effect of keeping Mommy in his room and out of his father's bed.

One night, after a few months of this behavior, John asked his mother, "Do you remember the other day when I cut off my penis with a knife?"

His mother saw in this such a clear example of Freud's theory that she would have suspected him of reading the book if he had known how to read. "But you didn't cut your penis off with a knife, Johnny. You probably had a dream about it."

He insisted that it wasn't a dream, so his mother could only reassure him with the facts. "Well, your penis is still there, and you don't use sharp knives anyway. Nobody, *nobody* is going to cut your penis off."

A few evenings later, Johnny carried his baseball bat, long Tinker-Toy sticks, a toy rocket, and a paintbrush into the bedroom where his father was lying down. He placed these "phallic symbols"—these representations, in Freudian terms, of the erect male organ—on the bed next to his father. "Here, Daddy. These are yours."

The next day his relationship with his father started to

return to normal. He began adopting more and more of his father's gestures, language, and tones of voice. He was on his way to becoming a small replica of the man who had so recently been his rival.

Your little "Oedipus" will probably not reveal himself in such casebook-perfect terms. You may not even notice a change. It is certain that he will not "know" consciously what is going on. It might help your son resolve his conflicting feelings if you and his mother can talk to him about them. You can explain that Mommy is married to Daddy and that you both love him. And you can try not to feel jealous of, or threatened by, the little interloper.

Other than that, there's nothing really that a father can do about this phase, except to be aware of it. He has nothing to worry about as long as his confidence in himself as a man is firm and his relationship with his wife is loving.

Your son, from whatever unconscious motivation, will learn simply by observing, that his mother is already taken, and that the best idea is to work hard at being a man like his father. From this unconscious decision to imitate you, your son learns to be a man.

"Here, Daddy. These are yours."

A father plays a crucial role in developing *every* aspect of a boy's masculinity. Once, when a boy worked in the fields or the shop alongside his father, a man taught his son the specifics of a life the boy would later follow. Today, most men can directly teach their sons "masculine" activity only through sports, camping trips, home and car repairs, and the like.

This is the aspect of fathering with which most men are familiar, since they were on the receiving end of it in their own childhoods. Fathers tend to use such shared activities as teaching times, to drill expertise and goals into their sons.

Watch a Little League baseball game. Watch a father "playing" with his sons in a swimming pool. Watch a father letting his son "help" him with a household project. Too often you'll see that the demands the fathers make are so exacting and their attitudes so like a staff sergeant's that the boys come away from the "friendly interactions" wishing they'd never started. Worse, they may have the feeling that their fathers' standards are too high even to be met.

Dr. Irving Bieber, a psychoanalyst, is among those who feel that this kind of pushing toward an unattainable "masculine" ideal is one way in which boys are turned into homosexuals. Unable to be the athlete, or the lady's man, or the mechanic that they have come to believe is essential to the male role, they give up on being men at all.

"Tough" fathers rarely are blamed for their sons' homosexuality. Instead, the stereotypical background for the male homosexual has included a strong, aggressive, and possibly seductive mother and a passive, weak father. But, according to Peter and Barbara Wyden, authors of *Growing Up Straight,* there are many patterns leading to homosexuality. They report that overly demanding, vicious, or simply noncaring fathers can also produce homosexuals.

Now that homosexuality has come out of the "closet," it does offer a more viable alternative to "straight" maleness or femaleness. The Gay Liberation movement argues that homosexuality is not evil or immoral, and that homosexuals should not be socially or economically penalized for their sex preferences. Still, it is doubtful that any father *wants* to raise a homosexual.

Don't fret. The Wydens maintain that "fathers have absolute veto power" over homosexuality, arguing that "a constructive, supportive, warmly related father precludes the possibility of a homosexual son. . . . Sons must be able to admire and identify with their fathers," they write, " . . . to become well-adjusted heterosexuals." If you are a man your son can look up to, he will strive to be like you, provided you don't set unreasonable standards.

Instructions in male skills and chummy chats on manhood do little harm, but speeches are not the primary way in which your son learns to be a man. Policeman Dick Fogarty figures, "I have to set an example to my sons—an example of how to be a husband, how to be a father, and how to be a man."

He's right. By seeing the day-to-day responsibilities you assume and how you carry them out, your son will form an idea of what a man is supposed to do for his family. By the way you interact with your wife, you show your son how men treat women, and how he can expect to be treated by them. By the way you behave as a father, you show your son how to be a father himself.

This process of identification depends on a relationship of mutual respect and affection between you and your son. If your boy dislikes you or resents your inattention, he will use you only as a bad example and will grow into a pattern of manhood different from yours. A large majority of the men I've talked with, in fact, missed a great deal from their fathers or came to actually dislike them. They echo Dick Fogarty's comment, "I scrupulously try to avoid treating my sons the way my father treated me."

You don't form a good relationship with your sons just by being "a pal" to them, or by taking them to football games now and then. You show them that you respect them by including them in *your* work and activities, by listening to them, and by being willing to discuss and explain anything and everything.

Mark Thompson, a college teacher with one small daughter, told me that he was happy he had a girl rather than a boy. "I don't like to do the things boys are supposed to do, like play catch and fix cars," he explained. He's lucky he does have a girl, because he's missed the point of fathering a boy. As sociologist Leonard Benson reports the results of a study by psychologists Paul Mussen and Eldred Rutherford, "the most crucial determinant of masculinity in young boys is probably the father-son relationship, not any particular activity of the father." Benson adds: "The boy's perception of his father as a nurturant and powerful individual is the important thing."

If you are happy that you are a man, and confident in the various roles that you play, however you play them, then your son has a good chance of growing into a happy and confident man, too.

A Little More Puppy-Dog Tail

But what does it mean, "to be a man"? Boys, according to the old rhyme, are made of snakes and snails and puppy-dog tails. Those ingredients refer to more than the contents of the pockets of a male child. What happens to the puppy-dog-tail quality in little boys—that spontaneous and unashamed expression of emotion and excitement, that freedom to enjoy anything that will make a tail wag?

We carefully "socialize" it out of our boys.

Tough, strong, and fierce; smart and a bit dangerous; able to bear the burdens of domestic responsibility with the patience of a snail—that's how we try to make little boys grow.

Is it fair? Just as little girls need to know that their minds can function for more than deciphering recipes, so little boys need to assimilate some of the attributes we habitually call "feminine." To be more than a rat in a race, a boy needs to learn how to enjoy the pleasures of the mind and the senses for their own sakes. He needs to be able to admit and act on dependency, to develop characteristics of warmth, love, and nurturing.

Sure, mothers, grandmothers, and female teachers serve as models for the nonmasculine virtues, and they can impart their morals and values to the male as well as the female children in their charge. But, child psychoanalyst Selma Fraiberg notes, "Since the little boy acquires these values largely from women, he regards them as "feminine" and has difficulty in integrating them into his masculine personality."

Even if your son is lucky enough to have men teachers in grade school, he will get most of his values from his father. It is important that you remember that today's world, and still less tomorrow's, is not a place where a man who knows *only* how to be a tough go-getter is going to find much happiness. John Michaels, a businessman and the father of two, complains, "Since I was born, I was focused on being a 'success'—in the *outside* world. Now, it's frustrating, because I *want* to be able to be more involved at home, but it's a fight to admit it's 'important.'"

Training a boy only to be strong within a narrow "masculine" sphere may be inculcating ideals that are anachronistic. It certainly can lead to a life that isn't much fun. Leonard Benson reports that researcher Susan Gray "found that boys showing high levels of masculinity also had high levels of anxiety." If we can allow boys to keep wagging their puppy-dog tails every now and then, they may be happier and less anxious men.

As his model for masculinity, you owe your son praise for his expressive qualities—his warmth, love, sensitivity, and sharing—as well as for his instrumental and intellectual ones. He may have to learn to fight, figuratively and literally, but he can learn from you that fighting is a last resort, not an ability that's necessary to masculinity. You can help him channel creatively his natural needs for aggressiveness and dominance.

Sports are a useful outlet for male energy and aggression. They are fine, but a father needs to remember that teamwork, not winning, is the real point of a game. He should teach his son that cooperation, rather than competition, is gratifying in a world where competition really has led only to trouble.

You may be conscious of the need to avoid "sexist" comments to your daughter. But your son needs to be helped toward "personhood," as well. You can show that you approve, or don't disapprove, if he wants to learn to cook, or paint, or play the flute. You can refrain from the

Whenever you're about to say "Boys don't cook or snuggle babies," bite your tongue.

"Someday this will all be yours, son," or the "Son, I want you to go further than I did" type of comment that will make him feel he fails as a man if he doesn't follow your pattern of "success." And you can bite your tongue whenever you're about to say, "Boys don't . . . cry . . . cook . . . snuggle . . . play with babies."

If you don't work to raise a he-man, will you raise a sissy? No. Roles and sex characteristics are fluxing, and the future requires resilience.

Margaret Mead sums up the difference between "masculinity" and "being a man": "Masculinity is that part of a male's behavior which distinguishes him from a female—in his sex roles, in fighting, and in sport. Stress on masculinity means on *not* being a woman. But manhood is that part of a male's behavior which makes him a responsible human being, able to control his sexuality, bridle his aggression, protect and provide for his wife and children, and make some positive contribution to the world. . . . If taking care of children is seen as playing a woman's part . . . it will be looked at one way. If it is seen as an extension of manhood, as an extension of strength, imagination, and tenderness, it will be looked at the other way."

7

New Form of Fathering

Today we regard the dad who shares his children and the chores as a good father. Not long ago, he would have been accused of "playing the woman's part." Throughout the twentieth century, the American father has been working his way down from his pedestal. Until recently, commentators have viewed this trend as a "decline."

Centuries of habitual patriarchy created a father whose role was fixed and unquestioned at the time Freud started probing subconsciousness and superegos. Freud developed his psychological theories to fit a powerful father figure as seen in the nineteenth-century middle classes. Father around the turn of the century was assumed to be *the* disciplinarian, *the* value-giver, whose strong will was unchallenged and who had little interest, let alone involvement, in the care of his children. Freud's model became quickly out-of-date, as a survey of twentieth-century child-care literature illustrates.

Before 1930 or so, few experts gave advice about fatherhood presumably because the father role was so firmly fixed that a word to the wise seemed unnecessary. In the 1930's advisers on parenthood began to hint that the father was needed to discipline his children, to form their "moral character." After World War II, fathers were called upon to become really involved with their children. During the 1950's, we wanted Dad to be a "pal" to his kids, as if, failing in all other ways, a man might at least *play* with his offspring. The 1960's brought loud tut-tut's over permissiveness and the pal role. It was alleged, probably with some merit, that the violent youth rebellion of that decade could have been tempered by more discipline when the children were younger. Father's image had become pretty flabby.

A Look at Your Father—and His

How was it with *your* father, and with his? Among the fathers I talked with, there is a definite generation gap. The younger men, those born in the 1940's and raised in the 1950's, show a great awareness of the need for involvement. For the most part, they aren't too concerned with "getting ahead," having grown up with affluence. They suffered from having fathers who grew up without money and so were driven to try to earn a lot. Their attitudes toward their own families is, in part, a reaction against their "absent" fathers. They are also living under the influence of women's liberation and a concern for equality of roles. Some of them wonder if there's any point in differentiating "masculine" from "feminine."

The older fathers, born in the 1920's or 1930's, grew up with the anxiety of the Depression and of World War II. They became "go-getters" out of economic necessity and emotional need. They were parents in the days when Philip Wylie wrote about "momism" followed by Betty Friedan, who discovered the "feminine mystique." Motherhood was supposed to be an all-consuming commitment that swelled to the neurotic proportions of momism. Today, these older fathers either feel guilty about being too permissive or regret spending as little time as they did with their kids. They helped to blur masculine-feminine roles by turning the raising of their children over to their wives, and by failing to provide an authority figure. They were confused about trying to

94

fulfill traditional roles in a world where tradition had, in fact, already been scrapped.

Some commentators trace the "decline" of the American father to the commuting affluence that followed World War II. Others maintain that father first fell from power during the Depression, when, unable to play his basic provider part, he lost respect and status in his own eyes as well as his children's.

Sociologist Leonard Benson goes back to the industrial revolution for the source of Dad's decline. Citing John M. Mogey, he writes, "The most critical breakdown of paternal nurturance patterns occurred as the factory system was emerging in the seventeenth, eighteenth, and nineteenth centuries. . . . Overworked and underpaid, the man was no longer a symbol of authority, and often could not retain the respect of his family. Although women and children worked for low wages too, fathering stability was undermined more than that of any other domestic role as home and work were separated and men lost the historical basis for their strategic family influence."

With industrialization, and increasingly with automation and bureaucratization, the tools—father's symbol of his masculinity, the mark of his office as surrogate for society—were, in effect, taken out of his hands. As technology has progressed, a man's power over his own career and his pride in his own work product has decreased. Influence over his family and children has shifted from a man's hands into the arms of the state, through its health, education, and welfare regulations.

Freud paralleled the erosion of paternal authority with the decline in pervasive religious belief. Once, God was a father, and father was a god. As people began to question God the Father, they began to wonder about Dad's omnipotence, too. From autocrat of the breakfast table, to pal and garbage carrier, to—well, what *do* we think of you now, Dad?

The images we retain of father from literature of an earlier day are those of an impressive man, able to make the best of himself or to withstand the onslaughts of life. He tended to be stern, but just. He was the boss—a little old-fashioned perhaps, but usually pictured as being right. In more recent fiction, where father appears at all, he's more often than not pointed out as the cause of all the hero's hang-ups.

In comic strips and television shows, the prevailing literature of the 1950's and 1960's, Dad is either henpecked or a bumbling, ineffective fool, apt to do the wrong thing at the wrong time and saved only by the cleverness of his wife and children. In the television programs of the early 1970's father all but disappeared. Situation comedies were no longer about families, but about occupations. On dramatic shows, the men we saw as doctors, lawyers, or policemen may have been fathers, but we wouldn't have known it. When fathers stepped into the plots of these stories, it was only in a crisis situation, when a wife or child was sick or in trouble. It often seemed, too, that father was the one to blame for his wife's nervous disorder or his son's drug addiction. The one TV father of the early 1970's who stands out is Archie Bunker of "All in the Family." And what image does he convey? That of a man trying hard, in his loud and nearsighted way, to live by the old verities and the old roles, and failing resoundingly.

We recognize the reality in the Bunker image of the man with the paycheck who throws his weight around. But we want him to be "involved," too. We want a father to be a good enough provider to pay for the luxuries we think we need, but not to work too hard. He should be strong, but gentle; be a friend to his children, but still be the boss. He needs to cooperate with his wife in her traditionally feminine roles, but to retain his status as the chief value-giver and socializer. As Myron Brenton writes in *The American Male*, "father is supposed to fill the old roles in a new setting." Our confusion is understandable.

How Traditional Are the Traditional Roles?

Some of that confusion arises because of a misunderstanding of the "old roles." Was father ever a patriarch in this country? Fathers are required by law to be responsible for their families. In the Colonial days, and in some jurisdictions since then, children have been required by law, or overriding religious doctrine, to obey their fathers' commands. It is true that until relatively recent times, women were unable to hold property or transact business, and they are only now being given a fair economic shake or a reasonable chance of political success.

But Americans have always looked to their women for that "male" quality, strength. Women in folklore did almost as much as men to settle and tame the country. And American men have traditionally expected their women to work hard at whatever they were doing, whether plowing a field, or earning a few cents in a factory, or caring for a large and primitive household single-handed. In earlier times, it was only the upper classes whose women were put on a pedestal of refinement. Because of the strength Americans have imputed to women, we have given them much more power than they could have exercised under a true patriarchy. And, as Brenton writes, "patriarchy as it evolved in the United States is unique in regard to the power and responsibility it has assigned its women in the areas of child-raising and culture, in the shaping of the personality of the young."

Anthropologists recognize that within the formal structure of a given culture are many informal but effective channels of power and influence. American women have probably always been more dominant than the rules of society would indicate—and American men probably less. American parents have probably always shared more roles than their official images allow.

So when writers and speechmakers issue calls to "bring back the father," let us be clear about *which* "father" we want back. We *do* need a father who is more than an absentee provider. But we don't need an authoritarian patriarch, who wouldn't be effective in modern times, anyway.

In modern America we are beginning to ask some questions about what the male figure is supposed to do, to be, to represent. Our society has changed radically in this century. Yet many people still try to model fathers on old-style figures, or give them no role at all. Happily, among the young today many families are trying out ways of escaping the outmoded stereotypes. They are reshaping the old, rigid role to make fathering more effective, more rewarding, more creative—and more fun.

Do You Have to Win All the Bread?

"What's the main contribution you as a father make to your family?" I asked a cabdriver in New Haven, Connecticut.

"Me? I buy them things—and buy, and buy. And it takes two jobs to do it. The cab's only my part-time job—I work full days someplace else."

Did his wife work? No. Now that his youngest child was 11, didn't he think his wife might get a part-time job so that he didn't have to work twelve hours a day? Well, he didn't know about that. He sounded as though it had never seriously occurred to him.

Letting father off the hook labeled "provider" seems to be the hardest. And hanging him up in his breadwinning chores defeats some of the main purposes of fatherhood. When a man gets so that he's killing himself with overwork and not seeing his kids besides, it is time to look for a happier medium.

"No wife of mine will ever work," a man may boast, feeling that he will be viewed as a failure if she does. But these days, the *non*working wife is almost the exception. According to the U.S. Census Bureau, in 1970 *40.8%* of all married women worked, and *49.2%* of married mothers of school-aged children worked. They work because of financial necessity, because of a desire for luxuries, or because the job itself gives them satisfaction and a feeling of independence. But the advantages of sharing the breadwinning role, say those who've tried it, are greater than the extra income a working wife earns.

"My wife is a much happier, more relaxed person since she started to work," says a New York cabdriving father of four. "We should have done it long ago." His wife started to work part time when their first pair of children were in school. When the second pair arrived, she kept on working. "I think she's done better with the second batch," this 50-ish father adds, "and I think it's because she's out there and sees more of what's going on than she

"Hanging him up in his breadwinning role."

could have in a park or playground. She's not so wrapped up in them, so tired by them—she can appreciate them more."

Husbands whose wives start working find that they enjoy being with them more than before. "She's out in the world," says one, "and we can talk about the same things. She understands some of the problems I face every day." As Al Foster comments, "We have more to share. For one thing, Penny values money more now that she's earning it, and takes the budget more seriously. For another, we have the extra funds to do more of the things we both like."

Elizabeth Bott, a British researcher, found that the more a couple share roles within a marriage, the more rewarding will be their sexual relationship. This is no guarantee that your sex life will pick up when your wife goes to work, but you may reap some other unexpected rewards.

Sociologist Carl Ridley, after studying working couples, concluded that two happily working people are more happily married than if only one works. The more you share, the more you share. If your wife is home all day and you give her a hand with the house and the kids, the more energy she will have for doing the adult things you enjoy together, and the more interest she will have in what you are doing away from home. If you both are working, and sharing the household load as well, the greater the common grounds you will have on which to meet, and the more mutual pleasure in which to participate.

"Yeah, I'm glad my wife is working," Pete Morison admits. "Mainly because some of the pressure is off me. It seems like I'm getting more out of my job, now that I'm not worried about always having to get that next raise."

More and more fathers are realizing that they don't have to win all the bread. Many feel they need help, either to beat inflation or to be able to do the kind of work they enjoy. What about you? Would you be a happier man, a better father, if some of the providing pressure was lifted? Does your wife want to work? Do you know? You might be surprised. Receiving daily doses of liberation propaganda, she probably can't avoid the feeling that she's somehow wasting her time and talents scrubbing floors. It might do both of you good to encourage her to pick up a long-forgotten career or to try something new to stretch her horizons and your budget.

Staying Home?

You don't have to give up winning the bread to get more time and involvement for yourself and your family. Fathers I've talked with are making major and minor accommodations in their jobs and their ways of life. John Green took a job with less overtime and less traveling when his kids were old enough to know that he was supposed to be around. Lawyer Matt Lewis decided, when his wife was pregnant with their second child, not to press for the partnership that would have demanded more energy and time away from home than he cared to take. Electrician Joe Carter left an employer and set up his own office so that he could arrange a schedule that allowed for summers free to be with his family. Two male New York City schoolteachers got five-year paternity leaves from their jobs so that they could be with their preschool children.

A lot of fathers have simply set up shop at home.

When a neighbor's wife wanted to go back to work, he was against it at first. "I was making plenty. The extra money we'd have had to *spend* for her to work—for babysitters, clothes, carfare, lunches—just didn't make it seem worthwhile. But she was set on it. Said she was bored, couldn't stand the house. So we made a deal. *I* was bored, too. I'd always had it in the back of my mind to stop working regular hours and try writing free-lance. But Nancy worried about security—money for college and retirement. When she started work, I quit my job and started writing. Now we're both happy, and bringing in almost as much money as I was from my job."

Doctors and lawyers have worked out of home offices for years. Architects, artists, writers, accountants, carpenters, mechanics, photographers, storekeepers, repairmen—men of many careers could work out of their homes if they were willing to sacrifice a bit of "advancement" for a lot of involvement with their families.

"It takes a special kind of discipline," says one father who works at home. "You're there, but you can't be. At least with my third ear I can hear my children grow, and that's enough."

Herb Adams set up a studio at home and found it "difficult." "I'd lock myself in my room to make it clear I wasn't available, but I was still in demand by the kids. It was flattering, but hard to work." Some fathers have worked fine at home when they had only one child but found more than one hard to take. Those who tried are glad they did, because, as one said, "I understand my kids better, and they understand something about my work—and me."

If you are leery about even slightly shifting familiar patterns, take a look at some fathers who have really made a change. Mark Thompson works three days a week as a professor, and his wife works the same number of days as a computer program designer. Each takes turns caring for their baby, the house, and the cooking. On the days when their jobs overlap, a neighbor watches the child. Each enjoys both work and home roles.

Tom Klein has been a "househusband" for several years. Every morning he helps get his wife off to her job and his three daughters off to school. He is in charge of the house by choice, and he likes it.

Both Mrs. Thompson and Mrs. Klein work in professions where women get equal pay. Otherwise, such total sharing or reversal of function wouldn't be feasible, their husbands note. Also, both families have the aid of real or adopted extended families. Mr. Klein's mother lives in the same apartment building and helps with her grandchildren. The Thompsons belong to a babysitting co-op, and though that may not represent a radical departure from custom, it can grow into a sort of extended family, especially in the impersonality of the city.

Some young couples are forming and joining communes in an effort to recapture the closeness that "family" should mean; they search for ways of sharing the joys and the burdens of family living.

Social change requires flexibility. You may not be willing, or in practicality able, to take any radical departures.

But now that it's becoming common, and in fact challenging, for women to work, and now that paychecks often don't always keep abreast of inflation, you might consider sharing some of the breadwinning with your wife.

If you do, you should be aware that in a way you'll lose something by it. As we've noted, divisions of power in a family parallel income distribution. Your working wife will want and deserve more say in family decision-making, and you may have some trouble accommodating to what some men see as a threat to their status (especially if your wife earns a healthy salary). Your wife will want more help in carrying out domestic duties that were formerly her only province.

Sharing Your Home

Dick Fogarty says he does about half of the household chores. His wife might have disputed his percentages if she'd been listening, but he does take on a large share of the housework. She works part time, and he doesn't see why the work at home shouldn't be shared as well.

It's not unusual to walk into Fred Casper's kitchen in the evening and find him in an apron and rubber gloves, hard at work on the dishes. His wife doesn't *make* him wash dishes, and he doesn't particularly like it, but it is one contribution he feels he can make to help a wife with a busy schedule. John Green cooks breakfast for the family so that his wife can get herself ready for her part-time job and get the kids organized for school without having to get up too long before dawn.

No father with a wife who is sharing the provider role—the "man's work"—can expect her to do all the woman's work as well. Or can he? Too many fathers seem to expect just that. Hard as it may be for a woman to break into a man's field, it's harder to get a man to share the household tasks. Perhaps because "woman's work" is so well defined, and it is easier to accept a "masculine" woman than a "feminine" man. Or perhaps it's because housework is so damned tedious.

But relaxed roles mean sharing the bread as well as the cake. You needn't draw up a marriage contract or a weekly schedule (though some couples find it more comfortable to have it all spelled out). You could simply accept a little more domestic mess than you would otherwise like, or a little less fancy cooking. After sharing some of the housework, you might decide to hire help. Or you could send your shirts out. You can take the opportunity to do the chores you mind the least. Lots of men like cooking. One father we know thinks he does a better job than his wife with the dishes and gets a certain amount of satisfaction out of turning an awful mess into an orderly stack. Sharing your home means not hollering: "The baby's spilled some juice!" when your wife is in the den finishing a rush job. Clean it up yourself.

When it became common—or common knowledge—that fathers did help out with the household chores, at least one commentator expressed concern that such woman's work was beneath a man's "dignity."

By 1973 Dr. Spock had come to feel "that a father during the hours when he is at home . . . should put in as much time as the mother on child care, whether or not the mother has an outside job too. He should take on a fair share of the house chores . . . A father's participation in child care and home care isn't simply a matter of fairness to a mother—especially to a working mother. It shows her that he considers these jobs just as vital, just as worthy, just as challenging as his work in the shop or office."

To me, it does seem unfair for a wife who doesn't have a job to insist that her husband share all the housework. But "dignity" doesn't enter into it. If housework is undignified for a man, then it is undignified for a woman. Everybody hates housework, as a contemporary children's song goes, and it's less hateful and much faster if you can do it together. Fathers who allow and even expect a wife to be a co-provider are feeling the need to share the housekeeping role as well.

There's a certain amount of satisfaction in it. Not that housework can make you feel as happy as the soap-commercial women look, but it can put life in perspective and bring you closer to your wife. Closer through scrubbing? Well, sort of.

Just after John Michaels' son was born, the company

John worked for went bankrupt. His wife was on maternity leave from a well-paying job she loved, so he decided that, rather than get another job right away, he'd stay home and take care of his son and the house. After nine months as a "househusband," he was glad to go back to the office. His new role had offered the reverse of satisfaction, but it gave him insights into women's lives that he won't forget. "I recognized how much effort went into the care of the baby and the house, and I never again will put the burden of that heavy work on my wife. Until I stayed home, I didn't understand that feeling of being trapped, of being financially dependent on someone who, no matter how nicely, needed to be served."

It isn't exclusively "feminine" to wash dishes, and it isn't exclusively "masculine" to work. What is important is the spirit of cooperation with which each role is entered into. That sense of sharing is what your children need to grow up with.

Sharing Your Kids

The main regret of older fathers I talked to is that they spent too little time and effort in getting to know their children. The major reward that young fathers find in their role is the joy in watching their offspring grow and develop.

"You can't get close to a child who's presented to you all neat and tidy for a few minutes every evening," teacher Ed Zane commented. He, like many fathers, has participated in the nitty-gritty nurturing of his children, feeding and diapering his infants, chasing away nightmares, bandaging cuts, and going to PTA meetings. He is as much a parent to his kids as their mother is, and that is surprisingly rare.

More and more fathers these days are assuming what might be called babysitting chores. When mother needs a break, when she's working or out at a class or meeting, or just for the hell of it—you have the chance to get close to your kids. It is more than just babysitting—it is *time* together. A college dean takes his baby to the office with him. A businessman arranges for his 9-year-old to accompany him on a trip. A father takes full charge of his kids for a day or a weekend while his wife goes off to a conference.

Even if it's only for an occasional evening or weekend morning, minding your children and taking care of their basic needs can do a lot for you as well as for your kids and your wife. My husband accompanied Sean on his first visit to the dentist (I was chicken) and came back pleased to report that when the technician had asked at what age Sean had cut his first tooth, he'd been able to tell her. "Most fathers don't know that," she had praised him. But he'd known it because he had been on the front lines during those seemingly endless months before the first tooth broke through.

If you didn't spend long, intimate time with your children, you could miss that first chortle of glee when your baby discovers her toes. You'd never see the angry, frustrated tears over nothing that tell you what sibling rivalry is all about. You would never see that astonished glint in your son's eye when he suddenly understands something he's been trying to figure out and you took the time to explain. You'd never sense the tense pride that a daugh-

Inordinate pride in his children as shoots off his tree.

ter feels as she holds her father's arm walking to the movies.

Fred Casper took a lunch hour to attend his daughter's school picnic. He was proud that he was the only father there, and his daughter was beside herself with pleasure. Your kids cherish, probably more than any grownup can imagine, time alone with their father, whether it's at home, on outings, or at work. Sure, Mommy needs a break from the kids, and, hopefully, appreciates any relief you can give her. She will be a better mother if you can help her come home with a new perspective on her family. But to your kids, you are something extra special. One of a father's main functions—and rewards—is to mold his children's characters and personalities. Your kids will pay a lot more attention to you if they have proof that you really care, not only about their report cards and their misdeeds, but about them as individuals.

Bud Kreutz has four children. Only once has he served as a babysitter, and that was before the first had siblings. His advice to new fathers is to "never let on that you know or can figure out how to feed, diaper, or rock a baby." Although his wife works at home, he makes no contribution to chores or child care. He takes inordinate pride in his children as shoots of his tree, as extensions of himself. And yet, as his kids have grown, they have, understandably, had no interest in listening to his ideas, in following his advice, or in obeying his commands. Little wonder.

Sharing children means more than sharing child care. It means sharing them as people with their mother. It means sharing in the day-to-day joy of the sort only children can offer. When you get to spend Sunday running an electric train, or are warmly flattered by the service of a mud pie, "just the way you like it, Daddy," that's plain fun. And when you can share your own pleasures—reading, or hiking, or football, or birdwatching, or just walking around—with a fresh mind that is absorbing all you have to offer, you're getting a tremendous return on the share you've invested. Fathers, especially the younger ones, are realizing that their home and children are as much their own as their wives'.

"Woman's lib? I subscribe to the notion that it's people's lib," says Chris Scholl as he diapers his squirming son. "It's helped Mary have the courage to go after some of the things she wants; and it's helped me feel comfortable doing things—like this—that I wouldn't have missed for the world."

"New roles," Louise Ames of the Gesell Institute says, "*let* people try doing more things they want to. They don't *force* them into uncomfortable behavior." Anyone who thinks that women's lib is making women just like men, or feels that the blurring of roles will abolish sex and mark the end of the human race, misses the point. What really seems to be happening is not the women taking over from the men, not the men being cowed by the women, but women and men, mothers and fathers, establishing an increasingly mutual role in the upbringing of children.

Many experts fear the effects of any complete role reversal, arguing, with considerable justification, that men were made to be men and women, women. But roles don't seem to be reversing. The househusbands I talked with consider themselves, despite their unusual domestic duties, to be the fathers, the bosses. F. Ivan Nye and Felix Bernardo, in their book *The Family*, note that although they see greater role sharing, they find little role reversal. As Myron Brenton writes, "It should be possible to acknowledge the vital role of love and nurture that a man plays without . . . making the father's role seem peripheral and inconsequential." Parents who take the opportunity to become true parents, in work and at home, find that they and their children benefit from their mutuality.

When children live with parents who practice mutuality, they will not differentiate between such "masculine" or "feminine" traits as "daddy does the spanking and mommy does the dishes." We don't need that kind of differentiation. As our life-styles become more streamlined, thanks to labor-saving devices, work around the house will require even less time than it does today. The working world, from garages to think tanks, is being automated and speeded up. The four-day week, still a rarity, may seem like slave labor in your children's lifetimes.

If you raise your kids to view man's role as the sole provider and woman's as a birth machine, they are going to be lost in a future in which men and women will have time to develop as human beings.

Pessimistically, the future is going to be catastrophically confusing. Our children won't need to know what men and women are "supposed" to do. They'll need to know what each of them *can* do as human beings to make the most of the challenges to come. For no matter what the future is, it won't be like today, let alone yesterday. By watching you, they can learn that life is for sharing, not grabbing; that life is for cooperation, not competition; that the happiest people, male or female, are the ones who make the most out of their own unique lives. It is up to you to show them that the "new" family is not a patriarchy or a matriarchy, but a partnership.

Leaning on "Outsiders"

A father has other resources to draw on as well, if he is willing to make use of the times rather than fight them in the name of "tradition." As the twentieth century has progressed, increasing numbers of institutions have developed that have filled roles which, for a short time at least, we came to call "fatherly." Some may bemoan the fact that changing mores and developing social agencies have "usurped" a father's authority. If you think of these changes as "usurpation," you may imagine that your influence is eroding. But if you think of them as assistance, you will realize that they actually enhance your parental function.

Family counselors, mandatory education, policemen, psychiatrists, youth groups, scout leaders, working wives, child-raising texts—all recent social innovations do carry out the functions once reserved for fathers. And what's so bad about that? Nothing. After all, in more primitive societies, the extended family and the larger community joined together to advise the father and to bolster his authority. It is only our "modern" world that has expected the father to stand on his own as breadwinner, socializer, and wise counselor.

If your son is hooked on drugs, do you "diminish" yourself by turning to a professional for help? If your marriage is on the rocks, is it a sign of "weakness" to seek counseling? If your job keeps you from spending as much time with your kids as you'd like, are you "less of a man" when you suggest organized activities led by father-substitutes? Of course not—unless you consider it "weak" to take penicillin to cure your pneumonia. Services are available to help you and your family, and when you make wise use of them, you are fulfilling your responsibilities perhaps more surely than if you took the self-reliant, "father-knows-all" approach to life.

Not all these programs, whether they be welfare systems or psychiatric counseling, religious organizations or drug rehabilitation projects, are as effective as they might be. You'll need to pick carefully when you turn to them for help. And you'll want to support community efforts to improve them.

Some experts, like New York psychiatrist C. Christian Beels, see this "rationalization" of parenthood as a major trend in the future of the family. Others, like Alvin Toffler, author of *Future Shock,* predict actual professional parents: men and women who would be officially qualified to take over the job of parenthood from us fumbling amateurs.

Dr. Beels doesn't go that far. "Father is overworked at work, unable to give himself to full-time fathering," he writes. "His wife is fed up with full-time mothering. Both seem to want part-time work and part-time parenting." He suggests that we rethink what we've come to call "fatherhood" and recognize that it may be the function of both parents with the assistance of professional individuals and organizations who can provide preventive parenthood to keep children and parents out of trouble. As Beel writes, "Fatherhood is too important a function to be left only to the man in the family."

Forming a "new" family in a "new" society needn't mean finding free love in a commune, or living in the style of *Brave New World* or *1984*. Rather, it can mean facing honestly your own strengths, needs, and weaknesses, and drawing on the resources of the larger community to fill the gaps and reinforce the strong points.

3

WHAT'S A FATHER TO DO?

"The night you were born, I ceased being my father's boy and became my son's father. That night I began a new life."

HENRY GREGOR FELSEN

8

Whose Baby?

"To be a successful father, there's one absolute rule: when you have a kid, don't look at it for the first two years," advised Ernest ("Papa") Hemingway. Many papas less illustrious adhere to the same rule.

There are better ways to begin life as a father.

Dick Taylor was in the delivery room when his daughter was born. The obstetrician, new on the job, handed the baby to Dick first. "I've always felt that that simple act—or mistake—made a big difference in the way Dick has responded to Heather, and she to him," his wife, Sonya, says.

Dick hadn't noticed that the doctor's action was unusual. In most cases a mother is the first relative to see and hold the baby. The fact that Dick Taylor established physical contact with Heather the moment she emerged from the womb made it natural for him to continue that contact. From the first, Heather felt comfortable with Dick, and the bond between father and daughter is strong.

We adopted Sean. An agency caseworker presented him, a few weeks old, to me *and* my husband. He was *our* baby. The two of us stood on equal footing as parents from the beginning. Only recently, after I'd talked with a number of mothers, fathers, and other experts, did it occur to me that this agency ceremony, like the Taylors' delivery room experience, fostered a close father-son relationship from the start.

You may be grateful that your babies come out of your wife's body, not yours. But that fact can also make you feel like a second-class parent.

After a pregnancy that was difficult both for her and her husband Mike, Kathleen O'Connell gave birth prematurely to twins, who died almost immediately. Of all the friends and relatives who sent sympathy, Kathleen reports, only one expressed concern for Mike. "They all asked him, 'How's Kathy?' but not how *he* was taking it. It was as though those seven awful months and those two poor babies were only mine, not his at all!"

Too often, this attitude prevails even toward normal pregnancies and births.

Well, the thing swelling your wife's belly is *your* baby, from the instant of conception onward.

What Happens in the Waiting Room?

"How did you feel when your wife was pregnant with your first child?" I asked fathers.

"Happy," "proud," "excited"—those were the initial responses.

When pressed, some admitted, "Well, I did feel a little bit left out."

"I did miss things like regular meals, having my underwear washed. . . ."

"I was anxious. What if. . ."

". . . having a baby could cost me my wife."

A father who is only a worried outsider during his baby's first nine months of development naturally may feel at a loss when he first meets the infant. His wife "knows" this child intimately. *He* is a stranger, shy and maybe jealous. The more you can participate during pregnancy, the more like a father you'll feel after birth.

"Mary had her first baby the old-fashioned way—the

116

doctor did all the work," Chris Scholl says. "That time, I felt like money in the bank—nothing more. The second time, we did the natural childbirth thing. The course helped me understand the physiology of development—what was happening inside her. And after I helped with the labor, I really felt like a father. It was great."

More and more couples these days are having their babies together, through so-called natural, or prepared, childbirth. Many obstetricians now allow a father who seems to be calm, mature, and knowledgeable to be present in the delivery room. Some permit and encourage fathers to assist a normal delivery. What better way to "feel like a father" from the start?

Natural childbirth isn't for everyone, man or woman. Some doctors and hospitals forbid fathers to go beyond the waiting room. But the more you can understand what your wife is experiencing during pregnancy, and the more you know about what's happening to the fetus you both gave life to, the closer you'll be to your wife and your child.

Even if you are all in favor of the "old-fashioned," doctor-centered deliveries, you can get an early start on fatherhood by taking an expectant father's course at your hospital or Red Cross chapter. You can skim some of those books on prenatal development and infant care that fill your wife's shelves. You can accompany her on her visits to the obstetrician.

Your baby can come home to a father, rather than a stranger.

By the Book

And then what happens? Some fathers promptly become invisible. Until recently, child-care books have not discussed the possibility of a father's involvement with an infant.

Arnold Gesell's and Frances Ilg's classic *Infant and Child in the Culture of Today,* covering the first five years of childhood, made no mention of father. The U.S. government's *Infant Care* all but ignores the existence of Dad, too. Shirley Olofson, discussing "The Vagaries of Child-Care Books" in *American Libraries*, writes, "A curious underlying theme in many recent books on child care is that the father's role is completed at the moment of conception. [Dr. William E.] Homan does not mean to suggest to us that 'fathers need to be companions to their young,' but does suggest that 'the actual physical presence of the father is not nearly so necessary as . . . his strength and his backing of the mother.' If this view is to be accepted, certainly it can be advanced in the same way that the mother's role is completed at the moment of delivery."

In a Public Affairs pamphlet called "Making the Grade as Dad," Walter and Edith Neisser write, "Your greatest contribution to your baby is not in burping or bathing him, but in giving his mother the affectionate, steadying support which even the most poised and stable young wife needs at this time. If you give her what really amounts to 'mothering,' she, in turn, is better able to give the baby the feeling of security which will start him out right."

Your wife *does* need support—but if you are to feel like your child's father, rather than your wife's therapist, you need to get involved earlier.

It is true, as Louise Ames says, "Fathers vary . . . Some really take part—diapers and all. Others just aren't comfortable in a co-mother role. You should be the kind of father that is comfortable for you." But advice books that don't mention a father's role until a child hits the age of reason are like social-studies texts that begin the history of America with Columbus.

Feminists have objected, with reason, to advice aimed only at mothers, on the grounds that it oppresses women. Benjamin Spock, for one, has changed his counsel to meet such criticism. In *Baby and Child Care* he wrote, "the time for him to begin being a real father is right at the start," and then went on to define "real father" as making the formula "on Sunday" and feeding and changing the baby "occasionally." That kind of advice oppresses daddies, too. But to my question, "What's a father for?" Spock responded: "The father—any father—should be sharing with the mother the day-to-day care of their child from birth onward, I believe. This is a natural (unforced) way for the father to start the relationship, just as it is for the mother. Then no distance need exist, at any age, between father and child."

Treasuring the Trespasser

Treasure or trespasser? A new baby is a little of both.

Calling parenthood a "crisis," psychologist E. E. LeMasters noted that for a new father, too many bills, too little sex, and a restricted social life lead to a "general disenchantment with the parental role."

Your mother-in-law may have come for an extended stay to help with the baby. Or a nurse may be sleeping in your den. Who needs it? Besides all that, your wife may have forgotten you exist.

Not long ago, a young couple, still almost babies themselves, wheeled their infant through the park. The mother was continually fussing over the baby, checking it, arranging its blankets, cooing to it. Her husband stood forlornly aside, weighed down by his wife's purse and his baby's diaper bag. On his chubby young face was a look that said, "Why doesn't somebody take a little care of *me?*"

Customary ladies'-magazine wisdom would advise the little woman: "Try to pay more attention to your husband. *Pretty* yourself up and cater to him a little so he doesn't seem so unwanted." More productive advice: "Let Daddy *help.* Encourage him to adjust the blankets and push the carriage, not just be a beast of burden." The more and the sooner a father can get involved with his baby, the less lonely he will feel, and the better he'll be able to build a relationship with his child.

Some mothers are unwilling to let their husbands get too close to their baby. "When my sister had her baby," a friend reports, "she surprised the whole family by the way she *clung* to it. She'd been a real career woman, and when she had to take leave at the end of her pregnancy, she talked only about getting back to work. But after the baby came, she wouldn't let my brother-in-law near it. He could hardly even hold his own kid, let alone feed it or help out—and he *wanted* to."

"You're kidding!" a neighbor exclaimed when she heard the story. "Not me! I'll take any help I can get!"

Maternal overprotection does seem to be on the decline, but it still happens. One of a father's functions during infancy, according to psychologist Henry Biller and others, is to pry a baby loose to keep the relationship from becoming too intense. So if your wife gives you some excuse, like "You don't know how to hold . . . feed . . . burp a baby, change a diaper," make her show you how. If that doesn't work, read a book, or ask a neighbor. You, your wife, and your child need you to be close, physically and emotionally.

Some child development theorists maintain that, for emotional health, an infant needs the security of attachment to a single caretaker at first. Is there then a danger in too much sharing of the care of a young infant? Probably not. Few couples enjoy the kind of schedule that would allow them to share baby care equally anyway. But no father who wants to care for his infant need worry about being a threat to the baby's security. And more men are doing more caring.

As Edwin Nichols, a National Institute of Mental Health child psychologist notes, "Fathers no longer consider child care to be woman's work." The two male New York City teachers who won "paternity leave" to correspond with female teachers' leave of absence after birth did so to be able to "father" their babies. A few corporations are reportedly granting such paternity leaves.

New fathers who don't receive such official approval seem to be contributing more than their traditional share nevertheless. When Dick Taylor's daughter needed nighttime feedings, he would get up every time his wife did. "She was nursing, so I couldn't do that for her, but I'd stay with her, get her a cup of tea, talk to her and the baby while they were awake."

When librarian Kent Wilson's second child was born, he says, "I was pretty much in charge of Alice, the older one. Alice wasn't 2 yet, so my wife really couldn't cope with two babies full time. I fed, changed, and played with Alice. Sometimes I'd spell Nancy with the new baby, so *she* could give some mothering to Alice."

Guys like Dick Taylor and Kent Wilson aren't just giving their wives a break. Nor do they like having their sleep interrupted by wails of hunger the more because they "understand" them. And they don't look forward with pleasure to the sight and smell of a goopy diaper—any more than their wives do. But to them, baby care is a means toward the end of getting familiar with the creatures they helped to produce.

"The fact that fathers are generally less accepting of their children than mothers," sociologist Leonard Benson writes, " . . . is probably due in part to the limited bodily contact that fathers have with them during the first year." New mothers are sometimes alarmed by the lack of affection they feel for their babies at first. But even mothers can't love the little strangers until they get to know them.

Recently, evidence has been mounting that a father's *early* involvement may be crucial to some areas of a child's healthy development. Psychologist Henry Biller found that children without adequate fathering *during the first two years* have more trouble later, socially and academically, than children whose fathers were involved in their infancy. Biller also reports on studies indicating that the *first* two or three years of life may be crucial for proper sex-role orientation. E. Mavis Hetherington, investigating the effects of father absence on boys' sex-role behavior, found that if the father left *after* the boy was 5, the child's sex-typing was near normal, but if the father left during the *first* four years of life, the boy's sex identification was considerably disrupted.

Of course, no matter how important early involvement may be for you and your child, you may not be cut out for infant care. You may be terrified beyond all reason that you will drop the baby. You may have to gulp to keep down your lunch at the sight of a dirty diaper. You may not be able to sit still long enough for a baby to finish a bottle. Your nerves may scream every time the baby does.

If you can't keep your negative feelings under control, the baby will sense your attitude. Your face, your muscles, your voice will all convey your tension or distaste, and the baby may take the feeling personally. "This daddy person feels like he might drop me or throw me across the room. I don't think I like him." If information like that is to be stored away in your infant's brain cells, it might outweigh anything that is to be gained from caring for the baby.

A father who rejects the idea of meeting his baby's basic physical needs can at least strike up an acquaintance with the kid on walks and at playtime. Pushing a carriage or carrying a baby-backpack can let an infant know there's a Daddy around. Shaking a rattle will entertain your tiny daughter and make her want to reach out for it. Talking to your infant son will make him want to find out who you are. Throwing a big ball your new walker can catch is good for his motor development. Playing peek-a-boo with your 18-month-old will make her curious about you and give her a hint that you care for her. It isn't much, but it's something.

Still, care and feeding are worth a try, at least for a few bottles, changings, and rockings. You may find you like the look of worshipful relief you see in your baby's eyes, or the feel of a tiny warm body relaxing into sleep in your arms.

If you don't, you might ask yourself why. Do you feel that it is "unmanly" to be gentle and patient? It isn't. Are you angry at the intrusion the baby makes into your wife's time and your pocketbook? You would do well to talk out these feelings and try to resolve them, rather than make the baby the focus of them.

Or do you simply feel frustrated by the apparent futility of constant feeding and diapering? *You* wanted a kid you could play with and talk to, not a limp little machine that processes milk into mess every few hours.

A father may lack interest in babies and young children because he doesn't understand what they are about.

Every Pitch Needs a Windup

"Talk to fathers in language they can understand," Louise Ames of the Gesell Institute recommends. Guys couldn't care less about babies, she argues, but cars, say, or machines, they can grasp. On the chance that she wasn't underestimating the male mind, let's talk about cars. If, back at the factory, the engine parts of your car weren't put together just so, if the car wasn't given a proper trial run, if the dealer didn't tune it up quite right—you've got a lemon. A lot of hard and careful work has to go into a car before you can drive it out of a showroom. Once you start driving a car, you get the feel of it. You learn which jerks and sputters to take seriously and which to ignore. But you don't know how to deal with your car's unique quirks until you get to know it. It is the same with kids.

"My father wanted nothing to do with us until we were 12 and could carry on an adult conversation," Sonya Taylor said. But unless a father does some of the fine tuning early on, he's not going to have a kid who can carry on a conversation—at least not with him.

You wouldn't dream of accelerating your car on a cold morning without warming it up. You wouldn't expect to score a strike in bowling by just standing at the end of the alley and dropping the ball. You'd be surprised if you could hit a golf ball without addressing it first. Every pitch needs a windup, and every child needs fathering while it's still little more than a blob.

Your new baby may *look* and *feel* like a blob. But a baby is learning from the moment of birth, if not before. At first this learning is almost completely sensual. Babies literally get the feel of the world from the people who care for them. The mouth is the primary input for information during the first weeks and months. Hands don't grasp, eyes don't focus too well, hearing may be fuzzy, and even the nerve endings are still numb. But feeding is all-important.

As your daughter sucks on her bottle, she looks up at your face, and perhaps reaches out for it. It is different from Mommy's. It is bigger and scratchier, framed by less (or more) hair. Waiting against your shoulder for a burp, your son feels a different kind of body under him, a different hand at his back.

Their little minds aren't quite sure who this different person is, but they'll begin to make the association that this other person—you—can be relied on to meet their

123

needs as well as the regular attendant. So your baby begins to love and trust you. Later, when eyes can see, hands can grab, and voice can respond, the better acquainted you both will get.

Young children's minds and bodies grow in stages. They may progress through the stages at different paces, and they may skip one or two, but in general, human development is an orderly, organized process. Babies turn their heads before they can turn their bodies, reach before they grab, stand before they walk. They need to have relatively confident control over their own bodies, and be secure in their own family circles, before they can be expected to branch out into a wider social life.

During infancy and early childhood, your children will pass through three of the eight "stages of man" psychologist Erik Erikson describes. Infants develop a basic trust of the world, or a mistrust. Toddlers gain autonomy, or develop a crippling guilt over their independent actions. On such early bases lie your children's personalities, their ability to cope with themselves and others. By the time they are 6, they are complex individuals.

Imagine a computer manufacturer saying to his research and development team, "starting now, with nothing, you shall, in six years, produce a system that can maintain itself, move, communicate, think, and comprehend moral and social structures." Technology and science fiction have yet to create such a device—but you can. Between the ages of birth and 6, children will grow to $5/7$ of their adult height. Starting out amorphous, they will take on the shape of miniature adults. Out of the "blooming, buzzing confusion," they will pull a mind that contains an almost incredible amount of information. It functions as a center for computation, reasoning (sometimes), and communication. They will be able to move their once-useless limbs in effective coordination. They will understand something about good and evil, fair play and injustice. They will know how to love and hate, how to manage themselves and others. Watching a child grow from a "blob" into a coping human in a few years is a remarkable experience. Helping it happen is even more exciting.

Maybe there is no way to convince some men that a baby is other than a bother or a bore. When children are mobile, even if they can't read a paper or bat a ball, fathers have little excuse for ignoring them. There are few things more charming than a fat-bottomed toddler bouncing stiff-legged across the room to clutch the leg of her Daddy, or than a 4-year-old engaged in a very serious discussion of life with his Dad.

Unless you want to, you don't even have to roll on the floor or fingerpaint to entertain and stimulate your pre-schoolers.

A walk to the corner mailbox with Daddy is a thrilling journey for a small child. A visit to the place where you work is something for your 5-year-old to talk about for weeks. When Dad is the escort to kindergarten and meets the playmates and friends, the excited pride in a child's eyes makes the trip worthwhile.

As your children leave the pablum and diapers stage, your involvement with them can be more closely geared to what you enjoy, if that is all you can manage. George Forrest found, for instance, that he didn't like reading storybooks to his young children. He does like to play with them and take them on weekend jaunts. Other fathers prefer reading to make up for leaving their little ones behind on excursions.

Chris Scholl says he likes to do almost anything—shopping, walking, biking, sightseeing—with his kids *one* at a time. Giving a child a feeling of uniqueness by taking him or her someplace alone, without siblings, is one special function a father can fill. An at-home mother must sit on the whole brood, but a father can make each of his children feel special.

If you like to play little-kid games, build with blocks and play hide-and-seek, fine. But if you don't, just about anything you like to do your preschool son or daughter will enjoy doing with you. Fred Casper's hobby is wood-working, and to buy peace and time from his 4-year-old daughter, he starts her on her own projects while he works. He isn't expending much extra effort doing something he'd rather not. She probably won't be a carpenter when she gradutes from nursery school, but she's happy to be included in something that Daddy is doing.

Fixing the car, mowing the lawn, rewiring a lamp—anything you can let your preschoolers "particpate" in—is valuable, as long as your irritability threshold is high.

To your post-toddling children you can give an important feeling—that they are grown-up. To your wife, little children are still babies. With their mother, they probably act more like babies than they do with you. Most little children seem to be on their best behavior with Daddy. It's a treat to be with him, for one thing. For another, they may suspect that Daddy won't put up with as much as Mommy will. Fathers listen to their children, converse in grown-up language, and explain things that mothers may assume they're too young to understand. The very fact that Daddy should want to spend time with them is enough to make kids want to work a little harder at being "big" boys and girls.

Daddy Says . . .

To young children, you definitely are the big fist, Dad.

You are bigger, louder, and more exotic than Mommy, so your word carries more weight. But please throw it around gently.

All children need limits within which to grow and explore, and little ones need narrow boundaries that are firmly and fairly enforced. At various points between infancy and school age, they will fight to expand their limits, and at other times, as you can tell by their particularly obnoxious behavior, they will ask for firm control.

Although you and your wife need to discuss and agree on the limits your discipline will set, more often than not, you will be the final enforcer of your preschoolers' rules. Your wife can use all her wiles and threats to get the kids to settle down at bedtime, but they will listen when you say, "It is time for bed. Stop fooling around!"

Toys all over the living room? Mommy may be on the verge of throwing them all out when Daddy says, "C'mon, kids, you know I don't like to sit in all this mess," and the toys get picked up.

You are a giant.

Being a disciplinarian does not mean being a bully. Continued corporal or other violent punishment instills fear, not respect, and can establish a pattern in these early years that will make a rewarding relationship difficult in the future. And remember that you are a giant compared with your kids. A smack, a bellow, or a shake from you can be devastating. Better to save the extremes of punishment for the extreme situations, when you really want to make a point.

In the subtler areas of discipline, too, a father needs to play a part. Toilet training is the major event of self-discipline during the early years. It is the first, and perhaps the major, disciplinary feat of childhood.

When your child is trying to stay dry and clean, it is only because Daddy and Mommy say it is necessary and desirable. So you need to be on hand to give the pep talks and the explanations, to express pride and pleasure over successes. "Let's call Daddy on the phone and tell him," Sean would say after each of his early victories over the potty. He wanted to be a big boy more for Daddy than for Mommy.

If you stay aloof from this all-important first encounter with the grown-up world that you represent, or if you express disgust over the process, you can hinder rather than help your child's self-control.

A dad disciplines, too, just by being around. Because you are there and insisting on your prerogatives, your small children learn to share their home and share their mother's attention. That is discipline as much as a table of rules or a spank on the fanny. Discipline is often silent, and it need never be loud.

Keep It Down

Some men carry superdaddy blustering too far. Lots of fathers are loud. Maybe they have to shout at work, so they keep it up at home. Maybe they can't shout at work, so they let off steam by bellowing at home. Maybe shouting is just an ingrained part of their vocal cords.

No one can ask you to change your personality, or to magically shrug off all your frustrations and become a calmer, quieter person just because you are a father. No one asks that you *never* lose your temper. Kids as much as anyone have to learn that people can get *very* angry—even at them—and still love them. But you may need to keep in mind that what to you is simply an authoritative statement, accompanied perhaps by a bang on the table, can come across as a terrifying tirade to a small person who hasn't had a chance to get to know you very well.

Fathers should keep it down, if they can, and when they can't, they should remember the effect they are having. At least, they might react only with amusement when their 4-year-olds suddenly start using the same shouting tone on them.

You may need to keep some of your other energies in check around small children. Most fathers like to rough-house with their kids, and most children enjoy it. To a baby, it is exciting to be handled in a different way. For a preschooler, roughhousing lets off a lot of excess energy and is an easy way to get and keep Daddy's attention. But it isn't all fun and games.

"I wish fathers would hold off on the roughhouse till their kids are older," a nursery school director says. "For some children it can cause problems. When I watch the more boisterous ones tackling and tickling the others, I see a glint of fear in their eyes. 'I do this because I'm afraid somebody will do it to me first,' one told me. I wish more fathers would channel some of their little children's energy into more productive and less scary activities, like carpentry, or blocks, or water play. The kids need time with their fathers, without a doubt, but some fathers need to use judgment in how the time is spent."

Part of the excitement of roughhouse for a small child lies in the thrill of risking danger. That danger can seem very real, even in a father's protecting arms. So watch for signs of fear and don't overdo the horseplay.

If a small child expresses fear or unwillingness about any activity a father is pushing, too often Dad pokes fun—"don't be a sissy," or "fraidycat." That or any other kind of teasing, when continued, can be a slap to your child's self-esteem. What you're there for is largely to polish up their self-images. Too much teasing can tarnish them. *You* know you're only joking, but they have no way of understanding that.

Airline pilot Harry Trent is a jokester. He likes to do shell games and "magic" for his young children. He plays tricks on them—shortsheets their beds, hides their teddies—as though he were still the star smart alec at summer camp. "The kids love it," he laughs. They don't. The kids are bewildered and confused by it. They don't understand the games Daddy is playing, but somehow they know they've been had, and they don't like it. Being laughed at, even in fun, makes them feel smaller and dumber than they are. Fathers should play fair.

Even the calmest and most thoughtful fathers should be aware that at times their little ones may be frightened of them. Some infants, between 4 and 6 months or so, suddenly scream in terror at the sight of their poor father. It isn't anything you've done, Dad, just a phase the baby is going through for a week or so. Boys in the Oedipal stage (Chapter Six) may reject their fathers or express fear of them. Some children, in their third year, have a hard time being with both parents at once, and may push one aside. And all children, at various ages and stages, have temporary preferences for either mother or father. A doting father might take such "rejections" personally. Don't—it is probably just part of normal development and will soon pass.

On the Lookout

Doting fathers take personal pride in their children's development. Just-about-average Junior pops a tooth at 6 months, starts walking at a year, says a word at 18 months and can read his own name at 4 years, and Daddy asks, "Is that normal? I mean, that's pretty good, isn't it? Junior must be terribly bright!"

Take time to ask, "Is that normal?" about behavior that *concerns* you. Fathers can start playing their "stepping-in" role early in their children's lives. If they've made themselves at all familiar with the patterns of development, they may spot a lag or aberration that a mother might try to ignore.

Does your baby respond to you and other stimuli after the first couple of months? Do your preschoolers seem able to cope about as well as their playmates? Do your little boy's fears make him hysterical even after you've reassured him? Does your little girl cling so tight to Mommy that, even at 5, she's terrified of leaving her?

If you sense something out of the ordinary, all you have to do is ask, "Is that normal?"

Fathers need to step in to help with everyday problems as well. You can watch for household hazards, for instance. When your baby is about to become mobile, it will probably fall to your lot, Dad, to install baby gates, nail down loose boards, build high shelves for tools and household chemicals, conceal or lift up electrical cords, and generally backstop your wife's efforts to babyproof your home.

The biggest worry for many of the young fathers I spoke with was that some harm would come to their children when they weren't around to protect them. Thousands of children each year *are* burned, poisoned, or otherwise injured in their own homes. You can help prevent such accidents by making your home a safe place for your young explorers. Mouthing, crawling, toddling, climbing, running—all can be hazardous. You need to make an environment where they'll be as safe as possible. For your children require all sorts of potentially dangerous activities if they are to grow from womb-curled infants into straight-legged 6-year-olds.

Letting Go, Slowly

The baby you had trouble relating to grows into a "real" child in an unbelievably short time. As your kids make their first contacts with the outside world, in the playground or backyard, then at nursery school or kindergarten, they need you.

You were the first "stranger," the first not-mommy in your baby's life, and you can help your little boy or girl deal with all the other strangers they meet as they grow toward school age.

"Did you play with Jason today? I like Jason. Maybe we can all go to the playground together Saturday."

"I want to see the pictures you painted in school. They are terrific!"

When Daddy expresses an interest in playmates or paintings, kids feel that such away-from-home activities are important. You may no longer be the only stranger in your child's life, but you are still the most important one. You are their protector even when they are on their own with playmates. They invoke you and boast about you. Your participation, however slight it may seem to you, in their play and in their school can smooth their transition from home into the wide, wide world out there.

9

Pulling the First Tooth–and After

"Hey Daddy! Guess what? My tooth is loose!"

Standing work-weary by the front door, you may be able to give only a sigh in response to that momentous announcement from your 6-year-old. Wasn't it just the other night you sat rubbing gin on her gum, praying for that very same tooth to pop through? And now what happens? Her baby teeth fall out, leaving too little space for the big ones to grow in. That means braces, and bills. A little booze on the offending gum won't be any help this time around.

"Gee, let me see, Betsy. Yep, it sure is loose! Keep wiggling it, and when it comes out, maybe the tooth fairy will leave a nickel under your pillow."

"A nickel! Mary Jane got a quarter for her tooth. *Nobody* gets nickels any more!"

"Well, I'll make a deal. If you let me pull that tooth tonight, I'll arrange with the tooth fairy for a quarter. But every extra day the tooth stays in, the reward drops by a nickel. Tomorrow it'll be worth 20 cents, the next night, 15. That's the way the tooth fairy operates in this house. What do you say?"

"Well, I'll think about it."

"My tooth is loose!"

High finance, delicate negotiations, competing social pressures, independent thought, an interest in justice—all these are part of the middle years—from 6 to about 12—of childhood. Freud labeled this time between the resolution of the Oedipal conflict and the onset of puberty the "latency" period, because the sexual drives he focused on appeared to be dormant during those years.

Your grade-school daughter may "hate" boys and be a

scratched-up tomboy herself. Your boy may think girls aren't worth speaking of. This aversion to the opposite sex, and to anything as mushy as love or romance does not mean that kids experience no sexual longings or sensations—many do. But they temporarily shunt aside this aspect of life as they concentrate on nurturing a conscience, exploring friendship, and coping with school.

Bent on breaking out of the family circle, at least during the daylight hours, they may seem to snub their parents. They want a longer leash, but they like to know that you are holding on the other end.

Don't Skip School

"What did you kids do in school today?" a father politely asks at the dinner table. "Nothin' " is often the response. School is the focus of your children's life. It occupies a great proportion of their waking hours. But it is more than a time-killer. In school, your kids lead their social lives, make their friends and enemies. They learn the seemingly unchanging laws of childhood and the rules of the adult world. They face the contradictory challenges of developing the best in themselves while learning to subordinate themselves to a larger group. School life offers the heady elixir of achievement and the bitter brew of failure.

School, in short, means a lot more than learning facts well enough to rate a certain mark on a permanent record. The three R's may be only a sideline to your kids' major experiences within the halls and classrooms. Yet if your participation in your children's school life consists only of a signature on a report card, then for all you know, "nothin' " is what goes on.

Teaching a child—instilling the intangible values as well as imparting the hard facts—was once under a father's exclusive control. Today, school determines what, when, and how your children will learn. You may be able to select a school, however, or at least have a say in how it teaches. Too few fathers do even that.

Bert Howard reports that he got a reputation for being a superfather simply by going to PTA meetings. "After all, it *is* a parent-teacher association, not a *mother*-teacher association," he says. "I was always about the only father at the meetings, but I'm darned glad I went. I learned a lot about what my kids were doing and supposed to be doing, and I got some of my own ideas about education across." Going to PTA meetings and school functions is one way a father can keep in touch with the way his children spend their days.

Listening is another. You can ask questions till laryngitis sets in, and still get "nothin' " in reply. Your kids aren't really trying to cut you out, or be disrespectful. Now that they aren't babies any more, they are working on their own sense of themselves. School is their world, and although you might not be unwelcome in it, they have trouble translating their daily experiences. A father who keeps his mouth open with questions, criticisms, and sound advice is less likely to gain admittance to his children's world than one who keeps his mouth shut and his ears open. Your kids will be all too eager to report their victories, and they need your pride. It is the gloomier side of school that your youngsters may be less direct about.

"Daddy, how do you spell dinosaur? Daddy, about how long ago did dinosaurs live?" You can answer such inquiries with an "I don't know" or with a recitation of the facts as you recall them. You can suggest that the student of elementary paleontology consult a dictionary or an encyclopedia rather than her father. Or, you can take the questions as an invitation to participate or a plea for help.

You don't write your daughter's dinosaur paper for her. You don't even have to get stuck for an evening, guiding her through the mysteries of reference books. She may simply be saying, "This assignment is just a bit beyond me. I need some reassurance that I *can* meet the expectations the teacher has of me." You can give that reassurance, along with some tactful, practical help, if your ears are tuned to the right questions and you know how to respond.

"Dad, what if a kid didn't know the answers on a spelling test and copied the words from the guy next to him?" That's not the kind of question that requests a tirade about honesty and the low wages of sin. It calls for some probing to discover the specifics. If you are a father with the time for a quiet conversation on the topic of spelling cheats, you can help your son put into practice some of the moral precepts you hope to communicate. Or you may discover unsuspected pressures and tensions that caused your son to copy from his neighbor.

You can keep in casual contact with your kids' school-work by expressing interest in their homework and projects. Even if they insist they're doing "nothin'," they will be pleased and flattered by your attention and will want to do all the better at their work. You will be keeping in touch with your kids *through* their work. A sudden drop in grades, for instance, may indicate a problem apparently unconnected with school itself. Fathers should beware of punishing a child for bad grades. Rather, in dealing with poor school performance, as with all problems, they should look for the cause of the trouble before dealing with the symptoms.

School—schoolwork, school friends, school competition—constitutes a testing ground for a child's self-image. The early school years are a time when your children will begin to form an idea about how they stack up against other people. Now, more than ever before, they need a father's praise and response to help them shape themselves. Sometimes, though, it may seem that they love you only for your driver's license.

Chauffeur and Chaperone

Your 7-year-old Suzy has a birthday party to attend Saturday afternoon at two. Bobby's Cub Scout pack is going on a trip at 2:30, and Kathy, your 11-year-old, has invited six friends over for a slumber party that night. As your kids get into the swing of school and start to meet friends who live farther away than down the street, you may get the feeling that chauffeuring and chaperoning are your main functions.

Friends are a big part of your child's school years. Playing, exploring, and fighting together, kids probably learn more about the world from each other than from anything you or their teachers can tell them. When they work up a stickball game in a vacant lot, they teach themselves about competition and cooperation as well as about the need for working to improve a skill. Younger children who play house are trying on roles they may later play for real.

By establishing the rules of a game and following them, kids learn to govern themselves and get along with others. A child who has been spoiled and babied at home will discover that her friends demand more open and independent behavior. A boy who is used to kicking his little brother around will find that his friends won't be bullied.

Your school-aged children don't need you to play with them. This is their world, an all-consuming fantasy universe that is an environment for trying out reality. You would be an intrusion if you tried to join in, but if you represent a strong, dependable, concerned figure to them, you are always there in spirit. They recite the rules you have set down about safety, violence, sharing, and boundaries, in order to back up their dealings with their playmates.

You will get plenty of chances to meet your kids' friends, and lots of opportunities to lend an interested eye and ear to their activities. You should make use of these opportunities. You are allowed to make judgments about your children's games and playmates, and you need to.

If your son spends every afternoon and weekend with a bunch of kids you think are wild or rough, for instance, you can step in. If your daughter is constantly closeted with girls who look as though they belong in high school, not elementary school, you'll want to pay attention.

You don't stamp down and forbid such "unsuitable" playmates. Instead, you might start talking about the situation, gently trying to discover why your kids enjoy the company of children you don't think much of. You may find that they feel the need of high-powered or ultrasophisticated friends because their own self-confidence is sagging. You would be surprised to find how just a few afternoons alone with Daddy, doing things they enjoy, can give them the confidence to get close to a few children of their own choosing rather than follow a pack.

You may notice that a child doesn't have any friends and seems unhappy about it. He spends most of his time alone, watching TV or just wandering. She prefers reading alone or baking cakes by herself to giggling with the rest of the girls. Maybe she's too fat or too skinny, too dumb or too brainy. Maybe he likes birdwatching and is surrounded by athletes. They need their father. By taking some time alone with them, you can help them sense the value they do have as individuals, no matter what their social "failings."

Time Out

In general, you can't take the place of playmates, nor do you have to. But you do need to spend time with your school-aged kids. How to spend it? If you like scouting, sports, concerts, movies, or other organized activities, and want to share them with your kids, fine. But what if you don't?

"In America we take it for granted that all fathers and mothers play, or should play, with their children and that this is always good for them," says Dr. Spock. "Children do usually profit from having parents who enjoy being with them, provided the parents are acting the role of parents at the same time. But there are many fathers and mothers—even in America and even quite normal ones—who don't play with their children because they don't enjoy it.

"In simpler societies where people live by hunting or fishing or primitive agriculture, and where there are no schools, a father will begin training his son in his occupation at an early age, and a girl begins helping her mother.

"So it is perhaps more natural for the child to be striving for an adult level of interest and performance—and for the parent to be helping him to reach it—than for the parent to be trying to be a child. But in our urban and industrial civilization where a father works on the assembly line or in an office this system wouldn't work, so there's more justification for a father to set aside a little time for doing carpentry or for tossing a ball with his children.

"There are opportunities for companionable activities that don't have to be invented, in housework and lawn work."

"S.I. Hayakawa calls shared work "the most precious gift a father can give his son." A father's time is more valuable to his children than a new toy.

Your children may need time out from their busy schedules. Time out with Daddy is a special time. A walk together to get a paper. Having Dad drive to the birthday party or the game. An afternoon or overtime Saturday morning messing around at the office. But any time you spend, working, playing, or loafing, with your children makes them feel more worthwhile than any $A+$ can.

In Self-Defense

"He's almost 14 years old, and he doesn't know judo, karate, *or* kung-fu," a subteen was overheard telling her girlfriend.

Oh my! We do live in troubled times. Some of us live in communities so troubled that we feel we must at least consider training our little children to fight effectively in their own defense. Some fathers, in more peaceable sections of the country, will teach boxing or judo to give a timid or "sissy" child "confidence." Such lessons in self-defense (really controlled aggression) may do little harm. But they avoid the issue. More important than your children's skill at martial arts is their feeling that their own selves are worth defending.

Being able to fight off a bully or a mugger is only a minor aspect of "self-defense." When your son's friends decide to ride a cardboard raft down the river, or climb the skeleton of a burned-out building, he needs to be able to say "no." When your daughter's chums form a pact to brutally tease a "stupid" girl or consider taking a joy ride in a strange man's car, she has to be able to draw the line. When the guy who hangs around the playground offers them pretty little pills that are "just like candy," they must be able to refuse.

To an adult, such decisions are just plain common sense. But your kids, no matter how sophisticated they appear, don't have the experience to make an automatic rational judgment under social pressure. You can't make rules to cover every possible contingency. You can only convey to your children, by your acts and your attitude, that they are important, and not worth risking for any silly thrill.

When they refuse to go along with their friends, they face ostracism as a sissy or a goop. Their self-images must be strong enough to withstand that fate worse than death. "My Dad would kill me if he found out," is a good excuse for them to offer their friends. What they are really saying is, "My Dad has confidence in me and my judgments, and I won't betray that confidence."

One means of fostering this kind of independence is an unexpected one—money.

Money Matters

"Nobody gets nickels any more." What kind of money do your kids get? And on what basis do they get it? It matters.

Some parents simply dole out cash as their children need it. Others don't let their children handle money at all, but take care of all purchases themselves. Some base allowance scales on the going neighborhood rate. Some impose fines as punishment. None of these systems really employs money as the tool for learning and independence that it can be for a school-aged child. As the family member who probably holds tightest control of the purse and the income, a father needs to participate in his kids' finances.

It is probably true that a nickel is no longer an incentive for pulling a tooth. A nickel won't even buy a pack of gum any more. But a 10-year-old, say, who demands a $10 allowance because all her friends get $10 shouldn't get her way for that reason alone. She needs to understand that incomes and life-styles vary from family to family. One isn't necessarily "better" than the other, but all families, she must learn, have to cooperate to meet their own needs as best they can. Children do require money of their own for the practical and social expenses they incur.

Properly handled, allowances can also teach a child the value of money, thrift, and the patience of saving for a future benefit.

Jim and Freda LeBlanc have three children, aged 7, 9, and 11. At the beginning of each school year the LeBlancs sit down with their kids and work out allowance schedules.

How much does each one need for weekly expenses? Julie, the youngest, has to pay only for milk at school. She gets a week's worth of milk money plus a little extra that she can spend for after-school treats or save for her own purchases. Nine-year-old Mark needs to buy lunch as well, and he is allowed more time after school and on weekends to wander with his friends, so he gets a little larger discretionary fund. Kathy takes the bus to school and has started buying her own clothing and other things, so her allowance is larger still.

The LeBlancs try to take into consideration the amounts their children's friends can spend, but they make it clear that, though they will give the kids as much as they can within reason, their funds are far from inexhaustible.

Once the kids get their allowances, they know not to ask for more. Certain household tasks pay a bonus—mowing the lawn, washing the car, cooking supper, doing the wash, helping clean the house, and other chores that would normally fall to the parents. Some chores are required without pay—keeping one's room clean, helping with the supper dishes, and emptying the trash.

When each child was born, Jim's parents bought a savings bond for them. These and the bonds the kids get each birthday are saved toward college. When a child receives a disproportionately large gift of money, the LeBlancs encourage them to put part into savings. Kathy has her own savings account at the bank. Otherwise, the LeBlanc children get no extra money, as a reward or an incentive, but what they get, they may spend as they wish.

When Mark decided he had to have a super-deluxe airplane model kit, his father advised him to save his allowance and made sure that there were plenty of paying chores available if he wanted to earn extra.

Since Jim and Freda are careful with their money, their children don't feel they are being cheated in favor of some whim of their independence. They learn to be responsible for their own funds and to put off an immediate small pleasure for a future large one.

Under a system like the LeBlancs', a child doesn't come to equate his own value in monetary terms. When a kid gets extra spending money "because you've been so good this week," he learns to quantify his own "goodness" or "badness" into dollars and cents. If, instead, he earns money for work he's done, he learns basic economics: work earns money, which covers expenses.

If Kathy LeBlanc got a dollar for every A on her report card, she would start striving, not for the satisfaction of accomplishment or the pleasure of learning, but, like a rat in a maze, for a concrete reward. Missing out on a prize would only compound her disappointment about her lower grades.

The LeBlancs are wise, too, in not withholding allowances or imposing fines for misbehavior. The allowance, having been thoughtfully worked out, is inviolable. When Mark refused to straighten up his room and balked at carrying out trash, his parents dealt with those problems separately. Since the only reward he received for those tasks was pleasing his family, the only meaningful punishment would be the displeasure of his family. His parents might legitimately express their displeasure by saying, "You can't go out to play until you've cleaned up your room," or "No TV till you've emptied the trash"—those are social punishments for a social misdemeanor.

Fines are ineffective discipline because they usually aren't appropriate punishment for the offense. It is one thing when every family member kicks a nickel into the ice-cream-all-around kitty for every swear word or bathtub ring. It's another to say, "Your room is such a mess, I want 50¢ of your allowance." Fines not only equate good behavior with financial worth, but they are an easy way out for a kid. "Okay—here's 50¢, now I can go out and leave my room messy!"

"My object all sublime," Gilbert and Sullivan's Mikado sings, "Is to make the punishment fit the crime." Fines are fit punishment for certain "crimes." If your daughter borrowed 25¢ from her brother's bank without asking, she should be required to fork over a quarter (perhaps with interest) immediately. If your son broke a window when playing ball in a forbidden part of the yard, the cost of a new pane should be deducted, in installments, from his allowance.

To be effective, punishment must follow the offense as quickly as possible, and the connection between the punishment and the offense must be made clear to the child. If your 9-year-old is hours past her due time getting home, a fine, or a spanking, or the withholding of dessert won't teach her to come home promptly. Telling her that she must come straight home from school for a few days will. With your explanation, she will understand that she has broken a rule and caused her parents great concern, and her freedom in that particular area will be curtailed. That will help her remember to use her freedom responsibly in the future.

If your son has thrown a tantrum that left the house a shambles, taking away his bike for a week is a silly punishment. Making him clean up the mess he's made and stay in his room for a while till he's fit company is sensible. If, on the other hand, he's been caught biking on a forbidden busy highway, then taking away bike privileges for a few days is appropriate.

About the only "crime" that should not be met with punishment in kind is violence. Sociologist Leonard Benson writes, "It has been monotonously reported that the more children are punished for aggression . . . the more aggressive they tend to become."

"I'm spanking you because you hit your sister and hitting is wrong," doesn't make sense to anyone, let alone a child. Violence needs to be countered by calm. Making small children sit in chairs for five minutes, or older ones go to their rooms alone after pummeling each other quiets the kids and lets them think about the misdeed.

Punishment, of course, is only a small part of discipline, but the way you handle it can make a big difference in the way your children feel about themselves. A child who is hit for every offense will come to feel as worthless as a punching bag, and will come to hate the bullying father who thinks so little of him. A child who is constantly shamed will feel ashamed of herself. But a child whose parents dole out disapproval reasonably, according to a scale of intensity, will learn justice and can internalize it into self-discipline.

Children who are allowed to go their own ways within definite limits feel proud of their ability to use freedom responsibly. *But you do need to set limits, and to expand those limits as a child grows.* You may not allow your 6-year-old to cross streets unaccompanied. Your 12-year-old may travel all over town, provided she gets in by a deadline or calls to report if she has to be late.

Kids need to understand that rules are enforced for their own benefit as well as for the family's well-being. If a young child needs eleven hours of sleep and has to get up at seven, then bedtime is eight, with no procrastinating. But if you set a bedtime just to get the kids out of your hair at an early hour, they'll resent it and resist the rule.

Some TV is fine, if it fits the child's and the family's schedule, but too much TV, or the wrong kind, like too much candy or soda, is bad for a child, so you set appropriate limits.

You can assign household tasks that each child is capable of and expect them to be completed, but if the chores are too difficult or unfairly time-consuming, you can expect rebellion or resentment.

The more you can take children into the rule-making process, the more they can learn to discipline themselves. Nine-year-old Harry was never allowed to visit friends on school evenings. He volunteered for a school project that required after-supper meetings at a teacher's house on the next block. "No," his inflexible father told him. "You know the rule, and you shouldn't have volunteered." So Harry lost out, and, resenting his father's arbitrary decision, was tempted to break other rules to get back at him.

Ten-year-old Linda was supposed to be in bed by 8:30, but she had started taking music lessons and couldn't do her practicing and her homework without working constantly, with no time for relaxation. When she presented her father with the problem, he listened and asked for her suggestions. "Well, if I could have some time, not as much as I used to, for just messing around after school, I'd promise to go to bed at nine without any fuss. Then I could do my practicing, too." Her father consented, and she kept her promise.

Your word should have authority around your house, but it needn't be absolute law. Your children have to dissent from your opinions if they are to form ones of their own. Some fathers are too insecure to brook a challenge to their authority. Some feel threatened if their kids talk back to them. You aren't the only person in your household who is allowed to express anger. You need to help your kids do it, too. If they feel they've been unjustly treated, or are just plain mad, they should know that they can let their anger out without fear.

A father whose sole disciplinary technique is, "I'm your father, so you will do what I say," may fool little kids, but will only look like a bully to his older ones. And, comes the time when his kids realize he is not the omniscient god of thunder, he will be stuck with a disciplinary gap that his bluster will be unable to bridge.

Give and Take

In *Father and Son,* Edmund Gosse recalls "the appalling discovery, never suspected before, that my father was not a God, and did not know everything. The shock was not caused by any suspicion that he was not telling the truth, as it appeared to him, but by the awful proof that he was not, as I had supposed, omniscient."

It is nice to feel like a king, but *you* know that you aren't omnipotent, so why pretend that you always know all the answers? Your kids need the strength and authority you have to offer, but they will value those characteristics all the more if they can understand that you are just a human being who is making the best of himself.

If you answer your daughter's questions about dinosaurs with a lecture on paleontology that her fourth-grade teacher will poke holes in, what have you accomplished? It's better for you and your daughter if you can say, "I don't know, but I'll show you how to find out."

Your children also need to learn that they don't have to agree with your opinions. If you have trouble taking backtalk, remember that it's good for them to give it. It encourages independent thought. It is perfectly fair, of course, to demand that your dinner-table debaters think through their arguments, make them courteously, and accept disagreement.

A father who is comfortable with give-and-take about such impersonal matters as dinosaurs, batting averages, and the daily news, is likely to be open with his kids when they ask him the important questions, like "Daddy, how do we make people?"

Sex Isn't Only for Mothers to Explain

By the time your 6-year-olds lose their first teeth, they probably have some general idea about how we "make people." "A lady and a man start a baby and the baby grows inside a special place in the lady until it's ready to be borned, then it cries and comes out," a 5-year-old sums up.

By the time they are sprouting their 12-year molars and are launched into puberty, they must have a considerably more detailed knowledge of the theory (not the practice) of reproduction. Their school will probably offer a basic course in biology, starting with the observation of gerbils or rabbits in kindergarten, and ending with a study of those gruesome charts of "the reproductive systems of the male and the female" in sixth grade. The school may even provide a more imaginative and useful sex-education curriculum. Great—but it isn't enough.

Even if your youngsters aren't ready for the fine details of the techniques of intercourse, they do need to have what *you* consider a healthy attitude. And this, they can get only from their family.

"Well, their mother is around more than I am," a dad explains, "so she takes care of the questions that come up." Sex isn't only for mothers to explain. If your boys and girls feel that you are embarrassed by sex, or afraid to talk about it, or able only to give a suggestive answer to a sexy question, they are going to be more confused about an already confusing subject.

Both parents need to answer questions openly, and both of you need to take opportunities to bring the topic up. If the neighborhood dogs are having an orgy, and your 7- and 8-year-olds are watching with timid fascination, you don't have to let your own embarrassment show. "They're mating—there'll be a lot of puppies around here in a couple of months!" can provide information, open up the floor to questions, and convey the idea that Dad thinks making puppies is as natural an occupation for dogs as making babies may be for people.

You may not need to sit down with your son and ritually inform him about the birds and the bees—he's probably gone way beyond that, anyway. But you do need to share with your wife and his teachers the task of imparting the facts of life to him. Because between the time that last molar pops through and the wisdom teeth get pulled, his body will be ready for sex in its more practical applications.

10

Before You Know It...

He slams every door in the house, plays his radio at deafening decibels, then hollers at his parents to keep their conversation down so he can hear himself think.

She runs from the table in tears over too many "prying" questions. "I wish everyone would just leave me alone!" Then complains that nobody cares enough about her to come find out what's wrong.

They are teen-agers.

Incredible—when just the other day they were roly-poly Terrible Two's. In his book *How to Parent*, Dr. Fitzhugh Dodson calls the terrible-two stage "first adolescence." In their third year children are trying hard to be independent of their parents, but are afraid of being too independent. So are teen-agers. Terrible twos throw tantrums at the hint of a "no" and hurl baby-talk epithets at their parents, but are devastated when Mommy and Daddy go out. Teen-agers feel the same opposing impulses. Terrible twos, with their "no's!" and "mine's!" are separating themselves from babyhood, working on a sense of identity. Teen-agers, too, are seeking a workable self-concept. By their third year, children are ready to try out their new bodies, learning to control those recalci-

If your teenagers were caterpillars....

trant sphincters and coordinate their limbs. Teen-agers also have "new" bodies to test. Two's and teens are contrary, unpredictable, excitable, and exciting to behold. The teen years last longer than the terrible-two period. At puberty begin physical and social changes more dramatic—and traumatic—than a 2-year-old's.

Metamorphosis Without a Cocoon

Puberty. The name derives from pubes, the hair that grows in the pubic area, or groin, of adult humans. As a stage, it officially begins with a girl's first menstruation and the first sign of sperm in a boy's ejaculate. Before these momentous events, a child's body begins to produce pubic hair or the other secondary sex characteristics of adulthood: breasts, underarm hair, chest and facial hair, descended testicles, changed voices and shapes.

Adolescence. The word comes straight from the Latin (the ancient Romans had teen-agers, too), and it means a time of "growing up." During this period, your children are becoming sexually mature. They are also growing away from you, creating their own selfhoods to meet the society they will find as adults.

Boys and girls mature at different ages. For legal purposes your daughter enters puberty at 12, though she will be pubescent, and perhaps menstruating, well before that. Your son legally begins puberty at 14, though he will show his first signs of maturation by about 12. Your children's bodies, however, follow only their own "laws." Kids have officially six years to move from childhood into adulthood, with adolescence ending at 18 for women and 20 for men in many jurisdictions. But it may take them years beyond those ages to tie up all the loose ends of growing up.

If your teens were caterpillars, they would spin themselves a cocoon and wait during those six years, until they emerged as butterflies. But people are not equipped for cocoon-spinning, although the metamorphosis during adolescence may be every bit as miraculous as a caterpillar's. So teen-agers and their parents must live through the agonies, joys, and surprises of puberty and adolescence and make the most of them.

"I'm glad Nature puts adolescence at the *end* of childhood," one parent said, "so we'd have some experience before it hit. It wasn't awful, really, but it sure as hell was confusing." It is a confusing time for your teen-agers, too. That's why they need a calm, stable, concerned father who understands what they are going through.

You can almost see their bodies change, they grow so fast. Beginning with puberty, boys and girls gain height and heft. Their bones grow heavier, and their shapes take on the curves and tapers of adult men and women. Their appetites, insatiable one season, may dwindle to nothing the next. With food intake and growth rate struggling for synchronization, their bodies may change from gangly thin to pudgy fat and again in two semesters. Teens can be infuriatingly awkward and clumsy— tripping, fidgeting, knocking things over—until they learn to coordinate the unfamiliar dimensions of their limbs.

They experience complex hormonal metamorphoses. The development of the reproductive systems to a point where girls menstruate and produce ova and boys ejaculate and produce sperm is only a small part of the total overhaul the teen-aged body undergoes. Governed by the pituitary gland, much of the endocrine system forms new patterns of production and interaction. Newly operative glands churn out stimulants to growth. Unfamiliar adult juices take away the protective odorlessness of childhood and make the skin coarser and, for a time, oily. The human body is a marvelous machine, but it still needs a shakedown time before the hormones ebb and flow smoothly and efficiently. Adolescence is a time for experimenting, for teen-agers' bodies as well as their minds. Flooded by new hormones that turn off and muddle together almost at whim, *they* are spasmodically turned on, off, and muddled.

These physical changes can frighten a child. Imagine yourself getting a hypodermic full of some strange substance that made your face and body change almost daily; that made you feel like a visionary one moment and a toad the next; that made you want to laugh and cry, shiver and sweat at once. You would be frightened, too. And you would want someone to explain what was happening.

Your teens need your help in understanding what's going on. Your daughter, no matter how close you've been with her until now, will probably want to keep her physical changes a private, feminine matter (though if she broaches the subject, she'll appreciate a frank, unembarrassed response). Your son looks for reassurance from the other man in the family that what is happening to his body and emotions is normal. He already knows intellectually about the birds and the bees. Now he wants solid facts about his hair, his shoulders, his testes, his sexual drive—or the lack thereof. His school, his books, his doctor, and his friends will provide information, sure, but he needs details and support from the person who has been his masculine model since he was born. You don't necessarily have to force time for man-to-man bull sessions (but if he gives you the chance—take it!). You just need to be around, to give encouragement and verbal pats on the back, and to answer the questions that you hear and sense.

"Dad, when will my chest be as hairy as yours?"

"Never, kid. A hairy chest is the sign of a he-man, and you just don't come up to snuff."

It was meant as a joke, but it was devastating. A teasing father can be anathema in adolescence. Your teen-agers require extreme tact about their budding butterfly wings.

"Well, Susie, I hear you became a woman today," one father congratulated his 12-year-old at the dinner table. She ran from the room in blushing agony and barely talked to her father for days. Such bodily changes may require explanation, but they don't need public comment.

Not only does their hormonal flux give them hair-trigger emotions, but their outward appearance may cause extreme concern. A girl who develops early may insist on wearing an undershirt over her bra so the other kids won't know. A girl who develops late may wear a triple A-minus cup over her flat chest so she won't be embarrassed in gym. A boy who can't control his voice may talk in a forced, husky whisper to hide the fact.

However sloppy and unisex the adolescent fashion may be, teen-agers of both sexes spend seemingly endless time studying themselves in the mirror. They *feel* so different, they must *look* different, and often they do. If they lag behind their friends in development—or race ahead of them—your kids need reassurance that everyone grows to average size and shape eventually. And they need to know that you like them, no matter how they look or feel.

Combat Zone

Admittedly, it often may be hard to like them, even if you do understand the causes of their behavior. Puberty and adolescence, in our culture at least, are stormy periods. Only a parent could love a creature who screamed at her mother at the drop of a dishrag; who berated his father for his lack of taste, sense, skill, and intelligence; who disappeared into the telephone for weeks at a time, with no word for the family.

Sometimes, the conflict within a home grows so intense that the children run away, or the family seeks help. One

153

teen-aged girl visited a psychiatrist at the request of her parents, who thought that her behavior indicated she was "sick." The doctor, after hearing about her difficulties with her parents, said, "Look, there's nothing wrong with you, unless there's something wrong with almost every other child your age in this country. You say you can't stand your parents. Of course you can't. If you thought everything was wonderful at home, you'd never want to leave it. And you *have* to leave home—that's why we grow up. So you tell yourself everything is rotten. That makes leaving easier, when the time comes."

Some friction is normal, but when it is extreme, constant, and unmanageable, outside help can de-fuse the situation. Teens and parents can benefit from individual or family therapy. You don't have to put up with uncontrollable adolescents, but you can't control them too tightly if you want them to grow.

Your teen-agers need to make an identity for themselves. To do that, they have to question every characteristic, every value you have given them. In their minds at least they will dissociate themselves from you and from the child they were. If you are calm, cool, and *there* enough, you may be able to see that they actually replicate you and your wife. Pointing this fact out, of course, will only spark another battle. For they have to make their own selves, even though, in later years, they may see that they were simply re-creating themselves in the image you had provided for them.

There's something else going on, too, underneath. "I hope that you will emphasize to fathers," Louise Ames urged, "how much trouble they can expect from their older teen-aged sons."

She is among many experts who point out extreme adolescent conflict between father and son. Some relate it to the Oedipal conflict. When your boy was 4, you were his rival for the attentions of the lady of the house. Well, as the father of an adolescent boy, you are again, at least according to the Freudian-oriented theorists. Now that your son's body is sexually functioning, he could, physically, capture his mother from you. But he knows he mustn't. He wouldn't think, consciously, of seducing his mother, but the urge may be there. You are his rival, and although he can't engage you in a joust for the favors of his lady love, he can fight you on every other battlefield. He can flout your authority. He can put down your body, your mind, and your income. He can argue every statement you make, beginning with "good morning."

But he fights with his mother, too, you say? That, according to the theory, is because he's resisting with all his subconscious might the temptation of even liking her, let alone lusting after her.

And your daughter? The intensity of her conflicts with her parents will probably peak at an earlier age than your son's. Her fights with your wife are egged on by the Electra drive to win *you* over, and they require your calm neutrality.

Authority, conservatism, the old ways—all these must fall, in every family, before the forces of freedom, youth, and newness. Why not just give up and let them have their way, since they'll get it anyway? Because they need something to rebel against. No boxer ever won the championship after training on a flabby punching bag. It has to have the resilience to bounce back if it is going to teach his fists anything.

Life in a Bull's-Eye

We have a friend who is addicted to causes, lost and otherwise. She's in her 30's, but she will take up the anti-Establishment battleflag quicker than a college student, even if the battle makes no sense and conflicts with her other causes. Her mother had a series of husbands, with long gaps between each one, and Kay for a time was raised in foster homes. She's a charming, intelligent, apparently well-adjusted person, but she will fight for anything against anyone. "Why does she keep marching in these nutty demonstrations?" we asked a mutual friend after Kay had gone off to a "save our antique trashcans" parade or some such thing.

"Why? Because she never had a father to rebel against, I guess," came the response.

Child psychiatrist Robert Coles wrote in *Family Circle* in 1973 that he was glad fathers resisted any temptation to bolt from their adolescent-filled homes. "Adolescents rebel, and it's better to have their rebellion centered on someone who's *there* and can deal with it. Otherwise, the feeling of rebellion has no special target and it goes out against schools and communities or any kind of abstract authority that's handy."

Your teen-agers not only need you right there in the bull's-eye, but they need to know that you will keep their rebellion within a safe range.

Cindy Joseph had always been a pretty good kid. A self-possessed, well-groomed, and generally helpful girl, she was the apple of her father's eye. At 12, the apple showed signs of decay. At 13, rot seemed to have set in, and fermentation was starting.

One evening when her mother politely reminded her of her agreement to help with the supper dishes, she balked loudly. "You seem to think I'm your slave. Well, I'm not. I'm not going to mess around in that sink to-night. I just won't—and you can't make me! I'm going over to Jane's and I don't know when I'll be back."

For Cindy's mother, this was one too many in a series of hostile engagements. Giving her husband a look of fury and despair, she retreated into the living room.

"Okay, Cindy," her father said, as calmly as he could, "what is this all about?"

"I knew you'd take her side—you always take her side!"

"That's not the point. The point is that we have a few rules here—not many, but a few—about cooperation and politeness. Helping with the dishes is one of your responsibilities, and being civil to your mother, no matter how you may feel about her these days, is another. Now. . . ."

"No!" his daughter interrupted. "I will not wash the dishes! I will not grovel before . . . before *that woman!* And I don't care about your stupid rules. I'm going to start making my own rules around here, amd I'm going out now."

"No, you are not. You're not going anywhere but to your room until you calm down enough so we can talk about this."

With a glare that challenged her father to mayhem, Cindy stormed to her room and slammed the door, pinching a finger in the process.

Mr. Joseph joined his wife in the living room on a morale-building mission. "Well, at least she knows her own mind. Just leave the dishes—I'll help you with them if the little spitfire doesn't come around."

Later, he went up for a talk with Cindy, who was still sucking her finger. He reminded her that she wasn't an odd case—that most girls her age thought their mothers were evil witches. "But," he said, "we still all have to live together. Now, if you think our rules are too tough on you, let's talk about changing them."

They made a deal. Cindy would be let off dishwashing detail if she would take on the responsibility for another job she liked better. "Well, I guess I wouldn't mind picking up around the house after school. Mom's not usually around then to hassle me, so I could do it on my own." "But what about time for hanging around with your friends in the afternoon?"

"I'd really rather be able to go over to Jane's or somebody's after supper."

"Fine. One more thing. You can avoid your mother as much as you want, but when you're around her, I'd like you to be a little polite. I rather like her, and it hurts me to see you being so rough on her. And do you think you could comb your hair and put on clean jeans at least when you visit your friends? I don't want people to think I've produced such a scruffy pup."

"Okay, Dad. I'll try—if *you* want me to."

From this and other similar scenes Cindy learned that her father would bend but not crumple under her onslaughts. She needed to know there was firm support somewhere, when she felt so shaky herself. She had the satisfaction of knowing that she could have her own way in "making her own rules round here," but she got the idea that a talk, not a tantrum, was the best way to do it. She had to rebel to cut herself free, but she didn't want to be suddenly let loose.

For Jeff Tompkins, the lesson was a harder one. When he turned 16, he was eligible for a driver's license. His father agreed to teach him to drive and help him practice while he had his learner's permit, on the condition that Jeff not drive anyone else's car or take any passengers until his father thought he was ready. Eager for the license, Jeff agreed. Once he got the license, though, freedom went to his head. He began badgering his father to let him go out on his own and drive his friends around.

Bob Tompkins refused. "You may have your license, but it takes a long time to get to be a good driver. I don't want you risking your own neck, much less some other kid's."

"Oh yeah? You don't really give a damn about my neck—you just want your high-and-mighty word to be law!"

Two days later Jeff was driving his pals around in a friend's car and smashed into a lamppost. Nobody was hurt, but the damage was considerable. Mr. Tompkins paid the expenses, since the insurance didn't cover an unapproved driver. He made Jeff pay him back out of his allowance and odd-job earnings, and took away his precious license for a while. He was wise enough not to say, "I told you so." He didn't have to. Jeff realized, without admitting it, that his father had been trying to give him about as much freedom with the car as he could handle, and that by flouting those old-fashioned rules he'd almost scored a hit on himself, rather than the paternal bull's-eye he'd been aiming for.

You may never have considered yourself the tough guy around your house, and you may have always shared the disciplining and decision-making with your wife, so you may be surprised to find yourself the focus of your kid's rebellion. But no matter what your family structure or household routine, you've been the one since your children were born who was bigger, louder, stronger, and more potentially threatening. So you become the prime target.

You may be tempted to get control of the teen-aged situation by pulling out all the stops on that power you've built up since they were babies. You might think you could absolutely end all the nonsense with rigidly enforced rules of order. It wouldn't do any good. You would only drive the rebels underground. They are big enough to cross streets by themselves, and they would simply disobey when they were out of your range. If, since infancy, they have come to like you and respect you, they will behave the way you want them to without being told.

158

If, instead of being the booming god of thunder, you are the calm in the eye of the storms that are raging within and without them, they will turn to you for support and guidance.

You don't want to beat all the independence out of them, anyway. Your job as a father has been to help your children grow, and now they are really growing.

Some experts theorize that adolescence needn't mean constant combat if a father has maintained a caring involvement with the children from birth. The closer the relationship, they say, the less need for revolt. A child whose rebellion is violent may be getting back at his father for years of neglect. On the other hand, as Louise Ames notes, an intimate relationship may provoke an even stronger effort to untie the family bond. And a smooth adolescence may hide a more serious problem.

While Alice Bertrand's teen-aged friends were ignoring their mothers and trying to topple their fathers, Alice had only good to say of her parents. All seemed so calm and friendly around the Bertrand household that Alice's friends got tired of hearing, "Why can't you be like Alice—she manages to get along with her parents."

After Alice and her younger brother had left home for college, their parents divorced. They had apparently been planning to for some time, but had maintained a front "for the sake of the children." When Alice was approaching 30, she suddenly exploded. She kicked her bewildered husband out of the house, broke communication with her parents, quit her job, and dropped into a completely new life-style. One of the friends she hadn't cut off commented after a session with her, "She's talking, acting, and feeling like a 13-year-old. It's as though what we went through when we were teen-agers, she has been saving until now."

That is exactly what she was doing. As an adolescent, she sensed the tension behind the front her parents had maintained, and she felt that if she took aim at either one of them, she might blow up the whole works. So she put off her rebellion. She was lucky that she was able to find a target for it in her 20's, because she emerged from her postadolescent metamorphosis a much happier, more relaxed, and confident individual. Some people whose rebellion has been quashed never get a chance to achieve selfhood. But if Alice had felt safe enough to cut herself away from her parents on schedule, she would have added ten years or so to a happy adulthood.

Ganging Up

The pubescent generation, first feeling the pangs of approaching adolescence, are card-carrying members of any clique they can find. Scouts, youth groups, secret societies, blood sisterhoods, after-school clubs are chic among the first-pimple set. As your teen-agers move further into adolescence, they may reject all such organized groupiness as baby stuff. They prefer to be "on their own," but with their own. They keep themselves well protected by their look-alike friends, by the current ikons of the youth culture, and by the telephone cord.

With their bodies and their feelings in such flux, teen-agers need some constants. So they dress alike, talk alike, listen to the same music, watch the same movies, go to the same places. They get their ideas from their friends and try out their own thoughts on them. This is normal. Our culture provides no formal rites of passage from childhood to adulthood. So our teen-agers create their own, longer ceremony, moving from childhood dependency to independence through an intermediate stage of social conformity. If you have confidence in your kids and have given them confidence in themselves, you needn't be too concerned about how they handle themselves in their social life. They may not lead the pack, but they know when to stop following.

Children whose fathers have not been involved and available may rely too heavily on their peer groups. They need the values of the group to fill the void left by fathers who should have guided them but didn't. The norms kids pick up from their peers may not be harmful, but they are based on less experience with life than an adult's (loudly though the kids may protest this fact). During puberty and adolescence, your children need their friends, their uniforms, their secret codes. Their quest for independence demands that you not be too intrusive or inquisitive about their activities. But they need a father who cares.

Keep a Hotline Handy

Dan Wilson was pretty popular in high school. He had a lot of friends, was on some athletic teams, held some school offices, and was generally considered a nice guy. He wasn't such a charmer at home. After one blowup too many with his father, Dan shouted, "You just stay out of my life. I don't need you!"

"So be it," his father, Joe, thought. "You'll see what happens." He was secretly glad to have an excuse to abdicate his authority.

Noses in the air, father and son went their own ways. When the next report card came in with lower grades than usual, Dan's father didn't comment. When Joe heard from another father that Dan had been dropped from the baseball team, he didn't mention it to Dan.

Dan was desperately trying to get the message across that he *did* want his father to be in his life, and his father was refusing to pay attention. But Joe Wilson had to sit up and take notice when the local precinct called him down to bail out his son, who'd been busted, along with some older guys the Wilsons didn't know, for possession of marijuana. Even then, all that Joe could think of to say was, "You see, you did need me, after all."

Communication with teen-agers isn't easy, but parents need to keep the lines open. Sometimes, all such "communication" requires is making your home a place where your teen-agers and their friends feel comfortable. Few fathers could honestly say that they *enjoy* having their peace and privacy shattered by the noise and clumsiness of multiple adolescents. But at least when the kids are at your home, you know where they are and who their friends are without having to pry.

If your wife too often feels the need to say, "Everybody out, Larry's dad is due home any minute," or "Hush, your father's trying to watch TV," your kids and their pals will migrate to another watering hole. If you are too gruff, too intrusive, or too uncomfortably pally with the kids, they'll go and take yours with them. But if you can put up with the inconvenience of having your home the center of your teens' social life, your kids may feel relaxed enough to talk to *you* once in a while.

Fathers who share time with their teens can maintain communication even if nothing deep is discussed during their association. You might invite your son or daughter to go places with you, just the two of you, or give them the chance to work (for pay) with you. They might often refuse (and you need to be secure enough not to be miffed), and they would resent it if you insisted. They'll know by the effort you make that you are interested in getting to know them on a new, more grown-up basis, and they'll be more willing to open up to you when the need arises.

You may have chances for man-to-man talks, father-daughter tête-à-têtes. If so, count yourself lucky. But for your hotline through their cocoons, rely on listening with your third ear and feeling with your sixth sense. Fathers must keep tuned in to their teen-agers, even when the kids tune them out. Adolescents may be just as incapable as 2-year-olds of asking directly for approval and encouragement—or of asking to be stopped.

The Other Facts of Life

Drugs, cars, alcohol, cigarettes—four of the tough facts of adolescent life. The Surgeon General might well label all these addictions "hazardous to your teen-agers' health." Yet all are central to American adolescence. Some stand as symbols of the yearned-for adult world. Some offer escape from the pressures teens endure during the "best years of their lives."

Every parent has to deal with these four facts of life, either as an abstract issue or as a practical problem. Concerned about the effects of these hazards, some fathers, even ones who are as mild as Clark Kent on other matters, suddenly become angry supermen. "If I ever catch you—using drugs . . . joy-riding . . . drinking . . . smoking—that is the end for you, my friend!" They add to the immediate problem an issue of discipline and almost challenge their children to step over the line.

A slightly better approach, if you feel the need to make absolute rules about these issues, is at least to explain the reason behind the rule. For instance, you can effectively expand: "Don't let me catch you with drugs." "Drugs can kill you. They can ruin your life. I won't lie—the thought of your ever getting hooked on anything terrifies me. It's a temptation I didn't have to face when I was your age. All I can say is, please don't get involved with them, for my sake and yours. If you do, and you're caught, I'll get you help, and I'll get you a lawyer but I won't get you off." Your teen might pay attention rather than automatically disobey.

And you have to set a good example yourself. "Smoking and drinking aren't good for anyone's body—but especially yours, where so much else is going on already," may discourage a teen from trying those habits. But if you indulge yourself, you aren't going to be too persuasive. "If adults drink and smoke, then drinking and smoking are adult pleasures, and I can therefore be adult by enjoying them," is just as logical as the purity pitch of a smoke-filled father.

Homilies and heart-to-hearts may have some impact if they convey the message that your concern is for your children's well-being, not your power. But they won't do any good unless, over the years, you've fostered your kids' respect for you and, most importantly, given them a good feeling about themselves. A boy who feels good about himself, or a girl who feels that her identity is worth finding, will have an active interest in self-preservation.

Drugs are probably the most terrifying threat to their children's lives that parents can imagine. They are especially frightening because few adults old enough to have teen-agers have had personal experience with them. And few parents know enough about them. A father (or a mother) can't avoid the topic and hope that it magically won't arise. You can't rely on the schools to effectively inform your children about drugs and give them the incentive to take care. You can't just hand a kid a pamphlet to read and heed. A crash program or big-stick policy *might* scare your teen-agers away from the drug culture, but it would more likely give them the added incentive they need to "show the old man" by challenging his law.

A father who wants to keep his children dope-free has to start early. This means being sure that he and his household don't abuse, overuse, or misuse *any* drug—be it aspirin, cough syrup, or tranquilizers. And it means that he must cooperate with his wife in raising children with enough respect for the integrity of their minds, bodies, and personalities not to want to damage them. With a life rich in experience, warmth, and acceptance, a child should have no need to trip out for sensation or escape.

And a concerned father has to be knowledgeable. He must have ready in his mind solid information about what heroin, amphetamines, marijuana, cocaine, hallucinogens—any type of drug—can do to a person's body, mind, and life. Not only that, but he has to *talk* as though he knows. If he thinks that "dropping acid" means "drinking lye," if he calls pot "reefers" and thinks an upper is a downer, his kids aren't going to listen to his outdated opinions. Listed in the appendix are books and other information sources about drugs. You need them.

A drug problem, like all the other behavior difficulties your child has ever displayed, doesn't exist in isolation. You have to face the fact that it is a *symptom* of other trouble. Nor can families isolate themselves from drug prevention. Your children may never get hooked, so you think. They stand a better chance of fulfilling that wish if you support community efforts to combat this new and frightening hazard.

Toward a Single Standard

Sex in a way is a "new" problem. We've always had it, thanks be. But from reading popular press reports about the sexual revolution, you might easily get the idea that no kid in the country is a virgin after the onset of puberty.

A closer look at the habits of high school and college students indicates that, despite the talk (and perhaps despite the envious imaginings of the older generation), the sex life of today's youth is probably not much different from that of their parents. Still, with the easy availability of contraceptives, and the widespread publicity about the techniques and ecstasies of sex, adolescent intercourse is a more realistic possibility than it was for the generations growing up before the "revolution."

So you can't deal with sex and your teen-agers as if the pill had never happened. George Forrest has a toddling daughter. Already he is concerned about how he will cope with his feelings when she's sexually mature. Remembering how he treated girls when he was dating, he says he "sees sex for girls as painful." That, combined with what he calls "an element of the father's image of his daughter as a perpetual virgin," makes him worry. "I'm sure I'm a male chauvinist pig, but I still don't know how to cope— it's the double standard, I guess.

Under that double standard, men have traditionally berated their daughters, "If you're not a virgin, how will I ever marry you off?" while advising their sons, "Do what you want, just be sure to use a rubber and not give your real name." Chortling over your son's wild oats and blanching at your daughter's just isn't fair or productive. With the coming of more honest sex and the development of reliable contraceptives, it isn't necessary. We can concentrate on the *single* standard.

"Don't hurt yourself, and don't hurt anyone else," the morality one Chapter-Four father hopes to impart to his young children, applies to your teen-agers with even more force. A daughter who lives by this standard during her adolescent sex explorations may not stay a virgin till she's married. She may not even marry the first guy she sleeps with, or the second—or any of them. But she may exercise some judgment in the relationships she forms and in "how far she goes" in each one. A son who accepts this value won't think of girls simply as "scores" or of bodies as objects to be used. He'll learn early to seek more than sexual relief from the people he gets close to. If we operated under such a single standard, a girl wouldn't have to be warned to be more "careful" than a boy. A boy wouldn't be punished less for his sexual drives.

This is not to say that adolescent sex doesn't have its hazards. And VD and pregnancy aren't the worst side-effects. Both can be cured, one way or another. But too-early intimacies can leave a trauma that lasts into and even through adulthood. Teen-agers are searching for a usable, honest identity. If they try to merge that identity too fully and too soon with another's, they can lose or warp their own. If they share their bodies before they have the feel of them, they may have a hard time getting close to themselves again.

But pregnancy *is* possible, and what's a father to do about it? Some parents and writers advocate the dissemination of birth-control devices to teen-agers. Others feel that such apparent approval of early sex is confusing for young people. Surely such a decision is up to you and your wife, in light of your own beliefs and your understanding of your individual children.

In most jurisdictions, doctors may not legally, without parental consent, help youngsters with birth control if

Premature pregnancy causes pain to everyone involved.

they are under a certain age. So you have the power to apply the brakes on too much experience too soon. Older teens can get and do pretty much what they want to when they want to. Whether you help them with birth control or not, by the time they've reached biological maturity, they need to have incorporated enough of your values into their own consciences so that they control their own lives and bodies reasonably wisely.

You don't have to threaten to throw your pregnant daughter out into the snow, or promise to disown your son if he knocks up every girl in town. But you can make it clear to your daughter and your son that premature pregnancy causes pain to everyone involved, including the unborn child, and that abortion, though legal, is not as simple, emotionally and psychologically, as pulling a tooth.

You probably can't expect teen-agers to behave as though the pill did not exist, but neither can you condone blatant disregard for the prevailing community norms. Promiscuity, among girls *or* boys, is another symptom of trouble. Kids who are "oversexed" are looking for warmth they may be lacking in normal living. They may be seeking an affirmation of selves they have no confidence in, trying again and again to "prove themselves" because they lack sufficient approval from other sources.

How about your kids? Do they need to find intimacy—and get back at their uncaring father—by sneaking around from one bed and back alley to another, living in terror (and secret hope) of being discovered and punished? Or do they pay you the compliment at least of turning to you, with little fear, for help after the fact?

Do any kids willingly report to their parents that they have syphilis or gonorrhea? Would yours? Would *you* have? Yet venereal disease is a real problem—medical, social, and psychological—with which your kids may need help. In many areas, teen-agers may go to VD clinics without their parents' knowledge. Some doctors routinely test for syphilis during checkups. Your children may not have the advantages of these services, or the knowledge of how to use them. Even if they do, they will feel more comfortable getting treatment if they know, by your comments and conversation, that you are aware of the problem and that you will love them none the less if they contract gonorrhea.

How to Hold Them

VD counselor, sexual adviser—these may be new roles for fathers. Helping their children plan education and careers is a traditional one.

All during puberty and adolescence, kids try on roles. One week, they may decide to be novelists and actually write a chapter. The next, they may yearn to be doctors until a volunteer stint in a hospital turns them off. They are going to be the greatest actors the stage has ever seen, till they get rejected for a part in the school play.

One of a father's tasks is to help focus these dreams and ambitions. As they advance through the high-school grades, your kids work toward a specific goal—either getting a diploma and finding a job, or getting into college. Which is it going to be? A lot depends on their own achievement and interests, but a lot depends on you. Your hopes for them can spur them on if they're ready to drop out. Your honesty with them about your finances can help without pushing your kids. Do they want to come into your trade or profession? They can spend time on the job with you. Are they interested in another field? You can introduce them to friends or colleagues who can fill them in on the details. You can go with them to visit college campuses, and help them decide if and where they want to go.

Some fathers make the mistake of bribing their kids to stay near home. "If you go to a local college, I'll buy you a car." It is scary to see your kids go away, but it is their life, now. As the old wisdom has it, you can only hold them by letting them go.

11

Full Circle

"When I was a boy of 14, my father was so ignorant I could hardly stand to have the old man around," Mark Twain admitted. "But when I got to be 21, I was astounded at how much the old man had learned in seven years."

It seems to take longer than it did in Twain's day for a father to "learn" anything. Our adolescence is stretched out, and what with college, army, or graduate school, a boy might not be independent enough to recognize his father's intelligence until considerably beyond Twain's 21 years. Many of the fathers I spoke with, even those who consider their relationships with their fathers to be sound, mentioned a very rough period between 15 and 25. Then the relationship smoothed out. What happened?

Man to Man

The roots of normal father-son conflict go back to the Oedipal competition and adolescent rebellion against paternal authority. But why should the problems last after these situations have cooled off? Chris Scholl may have put his finger on it when he said, "One day a father knows his little boy could beat him up—and fathers don't like that idea."

Picture yourself standing next to your father. You are about as tall as he is, probably taller. You are stronger, have more energy. You lack only his experience. You see in your father someone who has attained all he hopes for in life. You may envy him and may not be able to understand why you can't have all he has right now. Or, full of confidence that you can do better, you may despise him as a failure. In either case, the two of you are competitors. But you are used to thinking of him as your provider and protector. You still expect quarter from him.

Your father looks at you and sees his "baby." He may be proud that he has raised you as well as he has, or proud of you for growing so well despite him. He also may see a young man who can outfight him, outthink him, and show him up at his own game. He certainly sees a symbol of his advancing age, of the fact that his best work years are behind him. He may be frightened—of you and of what you represent.

You are both alone in a new world. It is natural in such a situation to want to hold on to familiar people, habits, and concepts, even though society says, "The child is grown now, so you both go your own ways." Confusion results. Parent and child resort to habitual resolutions.

Knots in the Purse Strings

We are familiar with the stereotype of the mother who cannot untie the apron strings, who broods over her middle-aged offspring as if they were babies. Why should it not be the same for fathers and sons? Often, it is different only in form.

Now that you are grown, what kind of demands can you make on your father, and what control can he exert over you? For many fathers and sons, the tie that binds is money.

Walter Troy's father had made rather a financial success of his work, and Walter grew up knowing the cozy side of comfort. When Walter left school and set out on his own, he had trouble adjusting to the financial status of a beginner. His wants surpassed his income, and he turned to his father for help.

"No," Al Troy said. "You're on your own now, and one of the things you have to learn is how to manage your money. I did it."

Walter resented what he viewed as his father's selfishness.

Though neither he nor his father realized it, Walter was not asking simply for practical help. He was seeking a sense of security that he missed, having left the well-feathered nest. Although he was expected to be his own man, he was asking for the privilege of remaining a child for a while longer. His father, on the other hand, was ready to relinquish the parent role. He saw himself as performing one last fatherly service, by forcing his son to grow up.

Some fathers continue to support—or provide extras for—their children long after the young have established their own homes. In their minds, they can remain the "cornucopia figure," and still may feel the rewards of being a daddy.

For other fathers, the daddy urge is even stronger. They are unwilling to release the control they have always held over their sons, and they use the power of the purse to continue to direct their grown children's lives. One older dad is reported to feel himself very generous indeed. "I told my son I'd be happy to pay if he wanted to go back to graduate school," he boasted, "as long as it was in engineering." Another father with a usually strong grip on the purse offered to make the down payment on a house for his married son. The house was right next door to his own.

Some fathers try to impose their wills through their wills. "Do and be what I want, or I leave all my loot to the neighborhood Home for Unwanted Cats." Others feel that they are being quite rational when they arrange for their estates to benefit only their grandchildren. To their sons, however, they are saying, "I wouldn't trust you with a cent, but I'm making sure you pay attention to me so you won't deprive your children." And they are saying to themselves, "I refuse to accept the fact that my son is old enough to handle my money."

In our culture, money is symbolic of so much—of esteem, of love, of the achievements of a lifetime. It may take you a while to feel confident enough of your own independence to say "no" to a parental gift, or to not ask for one. But you do need to remember, if you get into financial conflicts with your father, that the real question probably does not concern money, but a mutual need for dependence.

The Other Side of the Mountain

Not every son has these problems with his father. Not everyone has a father who has much of a purse to dangle by any string. But every young man whose father is living has a model of success or failure, either to imitate or avoid. Seeing the other side of the mountain the father has climbed may be enough to endow a father with sudden wisdom in the opinion of his grown son.

"My father, he thinks he's such hot stuff," a college student sneers. "What is so great about what he's done? I'll be raking in twice his income when I'm half his age." And then he finds, unless he has extraordinary luck, that raking in the income—or making great discoveries, or ruling the world—isn't quite as easy as it might have looked from his side of the mountain. So he must, grudgingly, give the old man credit for what he's managed to do. Father and son can then deal with each other honestly, as men who understand the same things, rather than as competitors.

"My old man? What a waste! He might just as well have never tried. I never thought he was dumb, but he sure didn't make the grade." And then the guy finds that on the job youth, strength, intelligence, even excellence may not make the grade. So he gets an understanding, after a few years away from home, that his father may not have been a "waste" through any fault of his own. And he may come to respect the effort his father made in simply not giving up.

Dick Taylor had never felt much hostility toward his father, but he had never been exceptionally close. "Then, when Heather was born—I was almost 30—I knew what it was like, being a father. I wanted to talk to my Dad, to tell him I understood what he had gone through, to have him share some experiences. By then, though, he had died, so it was too late."

Just having a child may have brought your relationship with your father into focus.

The Gift of Grandchildren

"I felt that Benjy was sort of like a gift to my parents," Art Robbins said. "It was as though, when we had the baby, I made up to my parents for all I'd done to them, and they'd done for me. The sacrifices they'd made, their worries when I was wandering, their hurt feelings about Jan and me living together unmarried so long—all that was wiped out because we had given them a grandchild. I don't mean it to sound crass, like tit for tat, or quid for quo. I just mean it seemed to make a tremendous improvement in our relationship, once I was the father of their grandchild."

Chapter One listed as one of the motivations for parenthood the fact that we are all socialized to want children. This aspect of our survival instinct carries over to grandparents. If a father gains satisfaction from reproducing himself, he is also pleased to see survival carried one generation further. Young parents sense this. George Forrest, feeling ready for fatherhood, planned his first child to arrive, hopefully, before his grandmother died. "I thought it would mean a lot to her to see the family being carried on."

We, and our parents, and theirs, take comfort in the concept of ongoing life. So grandchildren can be a gift that binds the generations. They can make a grandfather suspect that maybe his son isn't a ne'er-do-well after all. And they can make a new father feel closer to his own dad.

Grandparents, as we all know from myth and reality, are allowed to spoil and coddle a child, and criticize the child's parents. It is probably true that a grandfather has the time to play with his grandchildren that he lacked when his own kids were young. He has the patience, relieved from the pressures of parenthood, to put up with childish demands and behavior. Unburdened by

My grandfather taught me to bake pies and whistle.

mouths to feed and schooling to save for, he has the funds to spend on impetuous gifts.

But he also was a parent long before you were, and he may not be able to forget that fact. Grandfathers are not as notorious for intruding in the day-to-day management of their grandchildren as grandmothers are, but their influence is not always benevolent.

"Why is that kid of yours still wandering around in smelly diapers? When *you* were his age, I didn't put up with that nonsense." Your father is shaming your son, who has not yet been requested to give up diapers. You have to exercise a lot of tact. You can't stage a confrontation in front of the toddler, but you do need to take your father aside and explain a bit about *your* ideas of child raising.

George Forrest observed his father dealing with his son as roughly as Mr. Forrest had handled George, and he presented an ultimatum. "Either you leave that kid alone, or you're never going to see him again."

Hopefully, you won't have to take such an extreme stand. But you may need to enforce some rules. Too many gifts, too many disruptions of a schedule can be just as destructive for a child as the imposition of new or strange rules and values. If your wife feels uncomfortable criticizing her in-laws, it is your responsibility to see that your parents aren't too much of a good—or bad—thing for your kids.

"I know you're only visiting for a short time, but tomorrow is a school day, and the kids must go to bed."

"The presents are great, but we'd prefer them one at a time."

"When you bring a gift for Jimmy, please give Susie one, too—she feels left out."

"He'll get out of those smelly diapers when we feel he's ready."

You can learn a lot from your children's grandparents, too, believe it or not. Maybe you'll discover that the way your mother once soothed you works for your baby, too. Or maybe you can just take a cue from them and sit back and enjoy your children more. Seeing your kids through the eyes of their grandparents can make your offspring seem even more special than you had realized.

175

It is lucky that grandchildren can help smooth relations between fathers and sons, because your kids need grandparents—and for more than fun. They gain security and perspective from the feeling that their roots are solidly grounded.

"You are my little boy," you may say to your son, "and I am Grandpa's little boy."

"Grandpa's?"

"Sure, I was a baby, too, and Grandpa was my daddy. He still is my daddy."

"Oooh." Your son begins to feel that you are a person, too.

My grandfather taught me to whistle and bake pies. They aren't particularly relevant skills, perhaps, but I think of him, and his laughing patience, whenever I practice them.

Recently, we have tended to isolate the generations— the old into retirement communities and the young families into garden apartments or bedroom suburbs. But we all lose by such age segregation, and hopefully, the trend is reversing. One 80-year-old grandmother refused to move to a "golden-age development," saying, "I don't want to associate just with those old people. I like having young people, and their children, around—and I think they need me." Even at 3, Sean will point out a gray-haired person with a mixture of fear and pity: "She's a little bit *old*." I hope that he will grow close enough to his grandparents and their generation to learn that "old" people aren't for fearing or pitying, but for sharing love, knowledge, and opinions with.

Through "foster grandparent" programs that bring old people into contact with young, social-service organizations have shown that the generation gap can be bridged to everyone's benefit. Even if your own parents aren't available, you might find it worthwhile to make friends with some older people, in order to give your kids—and yourself—a feeling for the past as part of the ongoing present.

The highly mobile, tightly nuclear family of today may cut children off from their grandparents, and that's a shame. But we may not be so "nuclear" as we appear. Sociologist Howard Irving reports that married couples remain close to what he calls their "relevant family." Even if they aren't geographically close, most of the fathers I spoke with say they keep regular contact with their parents and other older relatives. Once a man feels he has made it out of his parents' nest and into his own, he seems to feel the urge to rekindle the fires of the larger family circle. This brings rewards, but it may bring added responsibilities, too.

On the Other Foot

"I couldn't figure out why I resented taking care of my father when he was too old to do it himself," a 40-ish dad reported, "until I realized that I just wasn't ready to admit that I was grown up enough to be parentless. Facing the fact that not only was I a big boy, but an old one as well, was scary. I guess I took my fright out in anger at my old man for a while."

The time may come when your parents require your help. Reversing the roles you've practiced since babyhood is hard. It's hard for them, too, to be dependent on their "baby." They may have been determined to remain independent until death, but circumstances forced them to turn to you.

You may not be legally obligated to care for them. You may not be financially able to. You may feel no desire to. But if the situation arises, you'll have to make some response to it, honestly balancing your needs, theirs, and your family's. If your parents can't care for themselves, they may have to move in with you, near you, or to a nursing home within easy distance. And then you are a father to your parents as well as to your children.

Some fathers steer clear of elderly relatives, saying that they want to protect their children from the illness, frailty, and death that surround old people. That may be an excuse for a father's own unwillingness, or it may be a sincere motive. But it is a mistake. It is true that older children may be irritated by the weakness and foibles of age (meaning anything over 35). But the lessons in consideration they can gain from being forced to be at least polite will stand them in good stead later.

And younger children often enjoy the role of helper.

Fetching Grandma's glasses, talking on the phone for Grandpa who is too deaf to do it himself—all the little services that grownups find annoying and exhausting, kids may like, because they feel so useful. "I may be a bother to everyone else, but Grandpa needs me." It is a good feeling.

The death of a grandparent may be your children's first intimate experience with grief and loss. They should be allowed to share it, to feel it, and to learn that grief passes, life goes on, and memory lasts.

It may be natural for a father to want to protect his children but it isn't wise or fair to cushion them too well against reality.

12

Part-time Fathers

In their book *Parents Without Partners*, Jim and Janet Egleson object to the term "part-time fathers." The end of a marriage, they point out, does not mean the end of fatherhood—even when the father does not have custody of his children. This is true. The divorced fathers I've talked with seem to have put more thought into their roles as fathers than the married ones. Because they have only part-time involvement with their children, they want to make that time count. Asking themselves, "How can I be a father to my kids even though I'm not with them?" they have found some answers to, "How can I be a father—period?"

What is it—one divorce for every four marriages? Statistics offer little comfort to the child and the father who must be separated because the parents cannot get along. How can a father ease what is at best a painful situation for him and his children?

Do You Have to Split?

"Sometimes an 'unhappy' home can be the worst thing for a child," family-life authority Eda LeShan comments,

179

"but it is not always worse for children than divorce." She feels that today too many couples use "the kids' welfare" as an excuse to break up over differences they once would have tried to live with.

Divorce is an accepted fact of life in America—perhaps, as Mrs. LeShan indicates, a *too*-well accepted fact. Politicians and professionals who once would have stayed married at all costs to protect their careers are now separating with the frequency of us commoner folk. Everybody seems to be doing it. You get a call from a friend you haven't heard from for a while, and intuition tells you, correctly, that he's announcing his divorce. You invite friends over to dinner and they call a day beforehand to say they can't make it because they've separated.

Calls to freedom echo around our ears. "Join the sexual revolution!" "Drop out of the rat race and swing!" Why not you, too? Your marriage certainly hasn't been the paradise of smiling cooperation and sexual bliss that a happy marriage "should be." Your wife is itching to be liberated. You've heard often enough how bad it is to stay married "for the sake of the children." So wouldn't everyone be happier if you and your wife went your separate ways?

Not necessarily. Not unless you are sure, down to your last ounce of conviction, that there is no other solution to the problems of your life. Divorce is expensive for fathers, especially when they have to maintain two households. And the life of a divorced father, say those who are living it, is a lonely one. Divorce may be socially acceptable and legally simple, but it is emotionally hard on everyone involved. It is only worth doing if your life together is honestly unlivable.

You would do well to try to patch up your married life before you junk it. Marriage counseling, family guidance, sex therapy, psychiatric treatment—all can be useful tools for repairing a marriage. Too expensive? Too embarrassing? Too time-consuming? Too painful? Probably less so than divorce.

You might also take a good look at the lives of the divorced fathers among your friends and associates. Does whatever swinging freedom they enjoy seem worth the emotional and financial cost? Ask them. After a few drinks, they might level with you. You may learn that *their* marital problems justified splitting, but that yours by comparison are nothing. The Eglesons write of a father ready to split who visited a divorced friend when the other man's children were visiting. He decided to make one more try at marriage.

You might separate informally for a while. Sublet an apartment or take a room in a hotel or boarding house costing about as much as you could afford for a long-term stay (not the poshest motel in town). Test your own reactions, and your children's. Such an experiment might give you and your wife just the motivation you need to work a bit harder at getting along.

Of course, such tests may only confirm your feeling that you have to separate. A marriage whose core has rotted out, in which the will to try has been exhausted, is not worth saving—and certainly not for the "sake of the children." Dr. J. Louise Despert, author of *Children of Divorce*, considers the children of an "emotional divorce" (a marriage held together despite irreconcilable conflicts) to be worse off than the children of actual divorce. Although children can probably weather more marital storminess than you might expect, tension, battling, and lovelessness create an unhealthy environment for them.

Children in such a home may be so fearful of shattering the thin ice of their family life that they withdraw into themselves and stifle their normal emotions. Parents who are too wrapped up in their own mutually hostile feelings cannot give children the attention they require. Children may know or sense that their parents are miserable, and may realize that Mommy and Daddy stay together only because of them. "Therefore," a child's unconscious logic runs, "I am to blame for my parents' unhappiness." The guilt can haunt them for the rest of their lives.

"Of course I considered not separating for my daughter's sake," says Steve Priestly, a 40-ish Midwestern businessman. "But you have to think of yourself first—then whatever is better for you is *really* better for the child. If you're happier apart, your child will know that, and she'll be happier for it."

If divorce is inevitable, what's the best way to handle it?

Keep Talking

Most couples wait until their decision to separate is final before telling their children. This is wise. If the matter is a topic for family discussion before it's decided, children are implicitly or explicitly made parties to the decision. That isn't fair. Children should not be made responsible for their parents' lives, and it can hurt them to feel that their opinion influenced their parents' split.

But divorce is in the air long before it is in the courts. The hostile silences, the forced pleasantness, the upsets, all let a child know that something is very wrong. You can get the problem out into the open without involving the kids. "Your mother and I seem to be having a lot of troubles these days, don't we? I know it's hard on you, and we're trying to work things out. I just want you to understand that it is not your fault. It has nothing to do with you." That kind of reassurance, even when it isn't asked for, can calm children's inner panic and prepare them for the separation.

"How did I tell my kids I was leaving? Let me tell you, it was hard," recalls Marv Winters, divorced for three years. "I felt like just packing my bags and leaving without saying anything, I was so scared. But I did tell them. I talked to the two separately and then together. I tried to be as honest and complete as I could. I tried to make sure that they understood that, even though I didn't care for their mother much any more, I did love them. I guess they had a hard time believing me, because I've had to tell them the same things over and over since then."

Children may need to hear the same explanations many times, and in many different ways, before they finally understand and accept them. Even if they don't ask, "Why don't you live here any more?" or "Aren't you going to be our daddy any more?" you still need to tell them. They deserve to know, and they may be afraid to ask.

No matter how small your children are, you should do them the courtesy of explaining why their family is breaking apart. Maybe they won't understand, but maybe they will. Trying to explain is a beginning that shows them you care, even if you do have to leave.

No matter how old your children are, they don't need to know the most intimate details of the breakup. Except in broad outline, your sex problems, money troubles, or psychological hangups are private adult business, not facts that even the most sophisticated children can incorporate into their ideas about their parents.

No matter what age they are, they don't need to hear something like, "It's all your mother's fault. She's crazy and she kicked me out." That may be completely true, but if they have to live with their mother, you as a parent wouldn't want to do them the disservice of making them hate the one person they must rely on for their day-to-day care.

"When I broke the news to my boy, I tried to do my trembly best," ad man Mike Sampson said. That first time and in all their conversations in the two years since his divorce, Mike has tried to emphasize to his 8-year-old the finality of the decision. "I have to cut off his hope and fantasy of a return." That is an important effort to make, even though kids may still fantasize about a reunion until they are grown or you remarry.

Most important—*they have to know that you are still their father, even if you don't live in the same house.* You can back this with an explanation of the plans you and your wife have made for you to keep in contact with the kids.

Depth Soundings

"What will the kids think?" is a big question in the minds of fathers who face telling their children they're leaving. How children react varies. A child who has always been up-front and open about emotions will behave differently from one who has always expressed feelings indirectly. Mike Sampson's son was quite honest about his protests and his desires to bring Mommy and Daddy back together. Steve Priestly reports that his daughter took his separation and even subsequent reconciliations and breakups calmly. "She seemed to understand."

Steve seems a thoughtful father with a close relationship with his daughter, so his judgment may be right. But a father needs to realize that separation or divorce is probably the first major crisis that his children have encountered. The disruption of one's physical and emotional environment, anxiety over one's future, the departure of a person one has trusted and loved—these are experiences that many adults have trouble enduring. Grownups under pressure may get ulcers or drink too much. Children have their own distress signals.

Most likely as the parent without custody, you won't have the chance to observe your kids too closely. But distance does give an advantage, and there are signs of stress that you can watch for when you do see your kids. A tense child may develop new nervous habits, such as nail-biting or twitches. You may notice sudden shifts in behavior: the usually quiet child who turns hyperactive; the outgoing child who becomes withdrawn. Frequent nightmares may be an involuntary symptom of fears and anxiety. Insomnia can indicate stress. Does your child seem to be gaining or losing extremes of weight? Stomach upsets or frequent colds can be invoiced cries for help. Has school performance suddenly dropped? A concerned father needs to watch for such unconscious messages from his children, and, if possible, to ask their mother for reports.

The tension may not surface immediately. Just as children need to hear explanations and assurances repeated *ad nauseam,* so they may take a while to work their worries to a perceptible threshold.

If you do catch signs of continuing tension, you may have to encourage your children to express themselves. Kids of divorced parents are often too well behaved when visiting Daddy. They may be afraid to express any displeasure, for fear, as one girl put it, "of driving him away completely." It is tempting to pretend, as *they* do, that nothing is the matter. It is healthier to expose even unpleasant emotions. "I sensed that my son was feeling quietly hostile toward me," one divorced dad said of his 10-year-old. "I didn't like it, but I could understand it. After all, as far as he was concerned, I had deserted him. I tried to get him to talk, but he wouldn't. So I kept talking. I told him I thought I knew what he was feeling, and that it was okay. He wouldn't say anything, but after a couple of weekends, he started roughhousing with me—I mean, wrestling hard. He had me pinned more than a few times, and he could *hurt*. I almost fought back, but I told myself, 'Hell, you've hurt *him*.' So I let him keep fighting, and I kept talking when I had the chance. After a while, he must have let it all out, because he started being more relaxed with me."

Extra outlets for energy, or extra babying and loving, may be all your kids need to be able to accept the facts of divorce. On the other hand, they may require much more help to resolve their conflicting feelings. If you are worried about your kids' behavior when they are with you, talk to their mother about it. Perhaps you should encourage her to take them for psychiatric therapy.

And how are *you* feeling? Many fathers, including those who have initiated divorce as part of a quest for freedom, seem surprised at the subsequent turmoil of their emotions. Divorced fathers need to admit and express their *own* feelings. When talking to his father about his new family situation, one teen-aged boy started crying. "Then I began to cry, too," his father said. "We just held on to each other and sobbed. I think it was good for both of us." It is always good for anyone to express emotions honestly. When the cause of the emotions is divorce, you may have to do some digging to get them out, and it may take courage to be honest about them.

After Mike Sampson's wife remarried, his son kept inviting him home for special occasions—birthdays, Christmas, and the like. "At first, I'd fudge—make up some excuse. Then I learned it was better to tell him straight—'I don't *want* to be with your mother and her husband.'" Such frankness expresses hostility, but points it in the right direction, *away* from the children.

Whose Fault?

"The children of the divorced are engaged too soon in love as a strategy," Herbert Gold wrote in *Love and Like*. "Joy recedes before strategy; these children are robbed of their childhood. . . ."

You can keep your children from being robbed of their

childhood by insulating them from some of the adult heat that divorce generates.

Divorced fathers carry a heavy load of guilt about "deserting" their children—and they may also harbor resentment toward the kids. "The guilt never goes away," as one man told me. But in the beginning, he reports, it was fierce—and confused. "I was deserting them, but mixed up with that feeling was the sense that *I* was being deserted by them."

The parent without custody is the one who loses his family, who has to start life over again alone, who has to fork out the extra dough for two households. If it weren't for the kids, he may feel, he wouldn't be in this spot.

"Everything was okay till the kids came along, and then the marriage just seemed to crumble—I don't know why," one father says. Whether it's the added attention a wife pays to kids, or the extra responsibility he isn't ready to take on, it is easy for such a father to unconsciously blame the kids for his predicament.

Or you may have agreed that after the divorce your kids would remain with their mother. It was a considered decision, based on sound practical and personal reasons. But the little gremlin inside you may be whispering, "Those brats stuck by that awful woman who ruined my life. I'll get them for that."

These aren't rational thoughts, but they may be natural feelings. So you find yourself forgetting your dates with your children, mislaying the support payments, bollixing up the arrangements for your time together. Those childish gremlins are powerful creatures, and they need to be faced down. Your kids didn't get you into this, any more than they asked to be born.

Shut Up!

It is all too easy to use the children to punish their mother (she may be doing the same to you). "The kids are wrecks after a weekend with their father," one mother complains. "He knows Janey's supposed to be on a diet, but he stuffs her with sweets. I've asked him to *please* see that they get to bed at a reasonable time, but they come home with huge circles under their eyes. One time, after I'd told him that Jack had agreed to save his allowance and go halves with me on a fancy chemistry set he wanted, he bought the boy an even fancier one. And I know, even if he doesn't say anything bad about me, he somehow gives them the idea I'm no good, because I always have a terrible time managing them for the first few days after they're home."

This kind of experience is what's called "using the children as pawns." Sometimes, kids are pawns during the divorce proceedings. "Give me the alimony I want or you'll never see your kids again." "Susie, tell your mother that you want to spend half your time with me. She'll listen to you." "Johnny, tell your daddy how hard it's been to buy the things you want on the money he sends."

Some kids are made to feel like spies on their parents. "Your mother's been going out a lot, hasn't she?" The divorced parents' rule of mouth should be: "If you can't say something nice about your spouse, don't say anything."

In other words, shut up! If your conflicts with your ex, over practical or personal matters, are too bitter to be suppressed, or if you suspect that she is bad-mouthing you, don't try to work it out through the kids. The Eglesons recommend using an arbitrator to settle postdivorce differences. This may be a hired person, a court-appointed one, or just some mutual friend or family member. Mike Sampson's former sister-in-law, for instance, is on good enough terms with him that she can serve as a go-between in his disputes with his ex-wife.

Alone Together

Shutting up is the least a divorced father can do. Cooperation with his ex-wife in a parent-to-parent relationship is the most. "After all, no matter what our differences, we're still the kids' mother and father," as one divorced dad put it. "We *try* to support each other in our dealings with the kids, and we almost always discuss the major issues—sickness, schooling, that sort of thing."

Father absence, as we saw in Chapter Four, can have bad effects on a child's adjustment and future. But if your ex-wife can verbally bring you into your children's daily life, they will have a father figure who is present in spirit, if not in the flesh. "I've talked to your father about this, and he agrees you should do it." "That's something you should ask daddy about when you see him." "Your father wouldn't like that—please stop it." When your wife feels comfortable invoking you, she'll have an easier time with your children, *and* she strengthens your relationship with them.

One father might say, "I know your mother has a rule about staying out on school nights, but let's go to the hockey game anyway." Not wise. His son may feel such guilt over breaking a daily rule that he can't enjoy the game. The boy may look down on his father for taking such a childishly obvious means to get back at his mother. Or he may learn that mother's rules are for flouting, and become impossible to manage.

A father who says, "Sure, it would be fun to go to the hockey game, but you know the rule about staying out late on school nights," may disappoint his son for the short term. But in the long run, he fosters the secure feeling that the child has two parents who care about his welfare.

If your children sense a spirit of cooperation between you and your ex-wife, at least where they are concerned, they will be more willing to come to you with at-home problems. Say your daughter has been having terrible rows with her mother. She may not want to mention them if she suspects you'll turn the information against your ex-wife. But if you've never used your daughter for that purpose, and have demonstrated that you share in responsibility for her, she may bring her worries to you for advice—and that is what a father is for.

Divorced parents need to work a lot harder at their roles. They may have strong feelings to stifle in the best interests of the children. But their kids still need both of them. Mike Sampson's wife remarried shortly after their divorce. "My son didn't like the guy, and was having a hell of a time getting along with him. I didn't like him either—and of course I was jealous of him for being with my wife and my kid when I couldn't be. But I had to swallow my pride and build him up to my son. I've tried to let the boy know that I am his father, and that I always will be, but that his stepfather is in charge at home and he'll manage to work both of us into his life." Mike has a tough job, but not any tougher than that of other divorced but concerned fathers. The role is easier to play if the script is clear.

Get It in Writing

The calmest, most rational people in the world can turn into infantile screaming monsters when they start working out their divorce settlement. A separation that starts out as an amicable parting of the ways can too often turn into a jousting match, with the lawyers serving more as cheerleaders than referees. Men who have been through it advise, "Get it in writing—especially where kids are concerned. Furniture is easy to divide, money is simple to arrange, but sharing the kids raises conflicts you would not imagine."

Your wife may be more than willing to have you spend all the time you want with your kids—but after the divorce she gets an uncontrollable urge to move to Alaska. "Of course you can have a voice in the kids'

The most rational people can turn into infantile, screaming monsters.

education," she says, meaning every word. Then she waits till after they are enrolled in boarding school to tell you about it.

Your life as a father will be much smoother if you make formal arrangements about the amount of time you want to spend with your children and the areas in which you want to retain some authority, as well as the expenses you take responsibility for. Unless you have some proof of predivorce agreements, you may find that the only way you can see your kids is to remove them bodily from their mother's home. Such a step might be dramatic, but it would open you to a kidnapping charge, not to mention the pain it would inflict on the children.

The time needed to work out such arrangements is a strong argument for long separations. A quickie divorce has great appeal. You fly to a sunny island for a weekend, and you come home a free man. But the longer separation time that most states still require allows you the opportunity to experiment with feelings, schedules, and needs. Until you have actually lived separately, you don't know how much money you can really afford to contribute. Until you've tried out various ways of spending time with your children, you don't know which works best.

Your Needs and Theirs

What does work best? "I used to think," John Green says, "that if my wife and I decided to divorce, I'd want to clear out completely. Make some financial arrangements, if necessary, but just totally break contact with her and the baby. Of course, that was when the baby *was* a baby. I thought that it would be easier on all of us if we got a chance to start fresh. Now that my son is older, I feel differently. For one thing, I'm a big part of his life as I couldn't have been when he was tiny. For another, I've had a chance to get to know and love him, and it would be impossible to leave him. I don't think now that we would split, but if we did, I'd be strongly tempted to fight for custody myself."

Kids need some father figure. And most men want to be fathers even after they have stopped being husbands.

So what do you do? Spend evenings with them? weekends? summers? And where? at their house? yours? a hotel? It seems common sense to recommend that life with father be as natural and homelike as life with mother. This means, for starters, having your children spend the night with you (and longer periods during school vacations) rather than just taking them out on the town. Having to visit your kids in your ex-wife's home makes for tense, stilted conversation. Even if there is a room with a door you can shut, or if your wife goes out during your visit, you are on her turf. Familiar surroundings can reactivate all the bitterness of the divorce. The optimal arrangement offers children a home away from home, where they can leave some clothes and possessions to keep their places while they are away from you. Although Steve Priestly needed only a bachelor studio when he left his wife, for example, he looked for a place with a small bedroom for his daughter.

For fathers who live in distant parts of the country and must travel to visit their children, a hotel room may be the only answer. Still, that isn't the best solution. It would be better to find some friend or relative who is willing to share a home.

Bill Paulsen and his children always spent weekends in the house of an unmarried aunt who lived near the children's home. She helped care for the kids and was more than happy to have the company. For a few weeks every summer, the kids visited Bill's apartment a plane ride away.

You have to work out a schedule to fit your own needs, of course. But the kids have to be consulted. If you insist on having them with you every summer, but they have always looked forward to going to camp, they'll only resent the time they have to spend with you. Flexibility applies to everyday situations, too. If your son's prom or scout camping trip falls on one of your scheduled weekends together, it doesn't make sense to force him to see you or make him feel guilty about skipping a weekend.

Some divorced fathers admit they feel almost as tied down by their kids as they did when they were married. "I'd think two or three times before accepting a good job offer that would take me out of the region where my kids are." "Yeah, seeing my kids sometimes cuts in on my social life, but it's usually worth it." If you demonstrate flexibility, you can ask for it in return. On the one weekend in the year when your new girl friend has access to a ski house, you might prefer to share it with her and put off seeing your kids for a week. If on occasion you've bent for them—and your ex-wife—they will bend for you.

In general, though, kids need to be able to depend on their fathers. Whether it is every other weekend, or the month of August, or next Tuesday at 6, they count on seeing you then. As their father, you stood for stability and reliability when you lived in their home. If you are to retain your status as a father figure, you need to be just as reliable now about keeping your dates with them.

Making It Count

Once you are with them, the routine should be as natural as home. Resist the temptation to be what one divorced dad calls a "superuncle." Presents every time, a schedule full of exciting events, all their favorite restaurant foods—these treats may simply be bribes to ease a father's guilty conscience. How much better, cheaper, and easier to plan one interesting event, say, in a relaxed weekend. If you do your own cooking, have your children help with the chores, and allow time for just hanging around and chatting, your kids will feel that you are their father, not their sugar daddy.

Many divorced fathers encourage their children to bring friends to their temporary home base, or to spend time with friends who have children. "I hope," said Steve Priestly, "that when my daughter starts dating, she'll feel comfortable enough here to bring her dates 'home' to me sometimes." He is one of several divorced fathers who mentioned efforts to get close to their own families after their divorces. Not only can your parents, aunts, uncles, cousins, and siblings make *you* feel more secure, but they also give your kids a feeling of continuity and roots as well. Every other kid has two set of grandparents, and your children are your parent's grandchildren. You all need each other. And your relatives, sometimes, can ease your "entertainment" problems with visiting offspring.

In planning activities, your children will appreciate having a say. You may have to pull suggestions out of them. Some kids are so afraid of alienating their fathers that they never say "no" to his suggestions. On the other hand, if you let them run the show completely, you are abdicating an important function of fatherhood.

Fathers are for discipline, and for being a firm but safe authority against which to rebel. "At first I couldn't bring myself to discipline my boys," one father said. "A spank was more than my guilty hand could do. Eventually, I had to, for my own sanity and theirs." Bedtimes, politeness, homework—whatever rules you would have enforced before your divorce, you must enforce after it. Then, when the time comes that your teen-agers start fighting back at you, you'll know that you have been a real father to your children.

Your Second Family

Being a family man without a live-in family is hard enough. Being a father to two families is quite a challenge. Bob Davis had a young son and daughter when he and his wife divorced. A few years later, he got married again, to a widow with three older kids. Subsequently, they had a baby of their own. After his remarriage, Bob had his children visit him in his new home. Sometimes, when he came to see them, he brought his new wife along. All these visits were painful for his first kids. His second wife was an all-right person, but she was a competitor for their father's attention.

At her home, they had to share their father with the older stepchildren, and later with the new baby. Sibling rivalry sharpened the conflicts they felt over their parents' divorce. They began to make excuses—even getting sick—so they wouldn't have to see their father in this new setting. Finally, their mother intervened. Bob agreed to take some of his vacation time alone with the children, and they promised to try to get along better when they

193

visited his house. The second Mrs. Davis was just as happy: two extra kids in the house, with a new baby, proved a strain.

When a father remarries, he has every right to build a new life, but he may need to make compromises in order to give his original family as much as he can.

"We Married Him"

Stepfathers wear the shoe on the other foot, but it may pinch, too. In the years after her first husband died, a neighbor says, her daughter Sally, by the tender age of 5, had gotten used to being "boss around the house." Then Ken came, and he thought *he* was going to be the boss. The going was pretty rough until they worked it out. "Partly, she was spoiled by having my full attention for as long as she could remember. But partly Ken was to blame. He wasn't used to children, and he expected too much of her. We'd all had fantasies—he about ready-made fatherhood, and we about how nice it would be to have a daddy. It took about a year to bring fantasy in line with reality."

As Sally put it, "*we* married him, Mommy." When you marry a woman with children, you do "marry" the whole family, so it is a good idea to know what you're in for, and to be prepared for a long period of adjustment.

Some stepfathers try too hard to charm their new children. The kids will sense the insincerity and resent it, especially if their father is still living. Those who have been fathers before assume that they know how to behave. Even if you've had kids, you have never had these particular ones. Ray Lander had three children before his divorce. He married a divorcée with two. In his first household, he had ruled with strict authority, but his stepchildren were used to liberal rules and a degree of democracy. When Ray started to throw his weight around his new home, the kids fought back, and necessary compromises took that much longer to reach.

Successful stepfathers recommend a slow and easy process. Get to know the kids, as well as the mother, as intimately as you can before you marry. When you do join the household, give everyone—including

194

yourself—time to get used to the new situation. Ask for pointers from your new wife about how the kids are accustomed to being treated, and stay a bit in the background at first.

Your stepchildren are like any small, strange animals. Rush up to them with open arms or clenched fists, and they'll either run or fight. Wait until they come to you and give you a good sniff, and they'll hop happily into your lap. You can't expect instant love or obedience, especially if they are still in contact with their own father.

But you have rights and feelings, too. You may have to draw the line at abuse, or stage a showdown to get their attention, if you are to win your stepchildren's respect. But don't fret. You have a new marriage to grow with— and that is hard enough, even without kids in the home. Building a solid foundation for your marriage is more important than trying to shape the kids right away.

Stepfathers, and divorced dads, will find in-depth advice in the books listed in the appendix, and from organizations such as Parents Without Partners, Single Parents groups, and Remarried Parents, Inc.

Uncle Daddy

No organizations exist to help the other kind of part-time father: the man whose job keeps him working late or out of town much of the time. These are absent fathers in an even greater sense than divorced dads, and their absence can be more devastating. Too often they don't make the effort that many divorced dads do to remain a father figure to their children.

If you seem to be away from home more than you are there, if you can barely recognize your kids when you see them, the first thing to do is ask yourself, "Is it worth it?" If the answer is "no"—do something! Your kids need a father more than they need the income you bring in. If the answer is "yes," there are many ways in which you can be more than "uncle Daddy," as one child welcomed her father.

Writing and phoning, regularly, to each child individually, keeps your children close. Some fathers and children record and mail tape cassettes for a more personal communication when they are separated for long periods. Your wife can collect schoolwork, report cards, photos, projects, and anecdotes to share with you on your return, so that you can keep up with the family's day-to-day activities. Try to keep your days at home uncluttered so that you and your kids have a chance to make up for lost time.

These are practical solutions to practical problems. But subtler conflicts may interfere with your father role. If your wife resents your absences, her complaining attitude may tear you down so that even when you are home, your kids want little to do with you. Talking the problem over may help, and bending enough so that she gets extra relief from her single-parent job will do even more good.

"It isn't the trips that are so bad," says one traveling widow, "it's the departures and the homecomings." So much emotional energy goes into preparing for the trip and recovering from it that the effective length of the time apart is stretched. "Everybody begins to get jittery about a week before my husband goes away. He's trying to get organized, and everyone in the family wants to get to him while they have the chance. There's more than a little anxiety on the order of 'what if something happens to him—or us—while he's away?' Then by the time he's come home, we've all gotten used to not having him around, and things are rough until we all settle down."

"My wife and I always seemed to have a lulu of a fight every time I got back from a trip," John Green reports. "It made me almost not want to come home, until I came to expect it and we learned to avoid it. Hard as it is, we try to put off any major discussions until after we've all had some rest and gotten used to each other again. And no fast-paced schedule of events till a routine is back in place." Good advice.

Allow extra time to prepare for a trip, so that everyone has a "last word," keep in touch while you're gone, and observe the formalities of a guest when you return. You'll be a father your kids are happy to see again.

Some fathers are forced to be "absent" by illness or disability. When such misfortunes keep a man from providing for his children, they can erode his status in his own eyes and his family's because we are all so used to thinking of the provider role as the father's main function. But it isn't, and guilt over not being the breadwinner can make a bad situation worse.

Instead, a man who is sick or injured can still be a functioning father *if he doesn't feel too sorry for himself.* A man who is bedridden can try not to make his demands intrude too much on the routines of his household and his children's lives. One who is ambulatory can lend a large hand in keeping the house and minding the children. If he doesn't demand too much special consideration from his kids, they'll relish having the extra time to spend with him.

Filling In

When Joe Keith's brother-in-law died, Joe volunteered to be a part-time father to his nieces and nephews. He has kids of his own, but he spends one evening a week at his sister's house and takes her kids with his own on weekend jaunts. They have come to rely on his visits and to turn to him for advice.

"It's tempting to boss them around when I feel they're getting out of hand," Joe says, "but except for maintaining order when we are together, I keep hands off. My sister's ideas about child-rearing are different from mine, so I don't feel right imposing my own rules." Sometimes, she refers her kids to her brother for "man talk." He serves as a masculine model for his nieces and nephews and backs his sister up.

All kids need a man to get close to, and many are missing out. An uncle, a friend, a grandfather, Mommy's boy friend—all can be surrogate fathers. If you find yourself in such a situation, it is important to remember that you *aren't* the father. You can control the child's life only indirectly. Once you do form a relationship with children, you need to do your best to be the kind of reliable, trustworthy adult their father would have been.

You may get a lot out of your part-time fathering yourself. One member of a single-fathers group who spends time with children without fathers comments, "We are all the less lonely for it."

13

Double-time Fathers

A judge grants a divorcing father custody. A single man adopts a child. A wife dies or is seriously ill—and Daddy must do double duty. Could you raise your kids alone? Most of the married fathers I asked said yes, they could—but it would be hard. Not only are there practical problems to cope with, but there may be emotional traumas involved—and fathers have needs and difficulties, too.

Taking Time

Al Bronston had a little advance notice that his wife, Kathy, would die, but not much. After he got the bad news, he determined to pull himself together "for the kids." A 36-year-old salesman, he had three children— Tom, aged 9, Lucy, 5, and Anne, 2. "I felt like the kids had enough trouble. They didn't need to see me collapse, too. So I told my boy when Kathy was past hope, and I let him cry a little. Then I said we'd have to be brave, but that everything would be all right. When she died, he was a big help in explaining to the little girls. I tried to calm them, to reassure them. I told them nothing would change, and I meant it. I didn't want a lot of sobbing relatives around. I didn't want strangers in my house.

"I got the time off work—the company was able to give me some sick leave with pay, and then they told me to take as much time without pay as I wanted. We'd had a life-insurance policy on Kathy, so I could afford to be without a paycheck for a while. But I did want to get back to work as soon as I could, for my own sake, and to give the kids the idea that life would go on.

"I'd get Tom ready for school, dress the baby, take Lucy to kindergarten, run errands and play with the kids all day. We'd had the maid since Kathy had gotten sick, and she took care of the housework and cooked supper. At first, everything was fine. And then, and then. . ."

Then what happened was that Al Bronston cracked up. He went into what his doctors called a severe depression and had to be hospitalized for a time. He was frantic about his kids, but his mother had come to stay with them and hired a live-in housekeeper who managed the kids and the house well.

Al learned the hard way that he couldn't be brave and stoic and be a father and mother, too. Few psyches can cope with that many demands. If your wife dies or leaves you, you have yourself to cope with first.

You may need time. You need to express and survive your mourning or your anger. You may need protection from your kids, or for them. Al was right in hoping not to disrupt his children's schedules. It is important in times of crisis not to move children or isolate them from their friends and routines. But a short visit to their grandmother, or a stay with her in their own home while Al collected himself, would have done more good than harm.

Taking Over

Death isn't the only way a man becomes a single father. Divorced fathers are winning even contested custody cases these days. It used to be that a man had to prove his wife to be promiscuous, alcoholic, addicted, sadistic, or any combination of evils to win his children, even if his wife didn't want them. Now, leaving one's children doesn't mean loss of face and status for a woman, who can find satisfactions in life other than as a mother. As part of the movement toward equalization of the sexes, many states have established "no-fault" divorce proceedings. New laws erase the automatic preference for the mother in custody cases, leaving each parent to stand on his or her own merits. Although some judges still follow the old truism that "fathers can't be mothers," more are recognizing fathers *are* capable of nurturing as well as providing.

But a man does need help, especially since we have not yet reached the point that a divorced mother without custody is ordered to pay child support to her ex-husband and their children. Somehow, a man has to earn a living and care for his kids. "I considered fighting for custody when we divorced," says one young father of two, "but it was just a fantasy. I simply couldn't have afforded it."

To win a fight for custody, a man has to demonstrate to the court that he is capable of caring for his children. He may have to present a plan for their care. How does he intend to be able to provide support for them while caring for their daily needs? Whom has he hired or asked to help keep house and provide a maternal figure for his children?

More single men are adopting children, too. With the great need for homes for older children, mixed-race children, war orphans, and children with problems, states and agencies are allowing unmarried people to adopt. But again, they must be able to show that they can insure the physical and emotional well-being of the child.

Widower, divorced, or adoptive father—how do you find the help?

Finding Help

First, a father has to examine his needs. A baby or other preschooler in the house requires more time and attention than older kids—full-time help at least, if not live-in. A long-term, steady caretaker is important not only for young children's practical wants, but for their sense of security, as well. Babies and toddlers need to become attached to one person who is always available.

To care for school-aged kids, you may need someone who comes in only in the afternoons, to straighten the house, keep an eye on the kids, and cook supper (though in order to find someone who is really good with children, you may have to hire another person to clean the house).

With older children and teen-agers to think about, it is tempting to do without outside help. In movies and other fiction, we revel in the idyllic cooperation of motherless children. They all pitch in to raise each other and care for Dad. Reality is not quite so jolly.

One young man whose mother was quite ill during his adolescence was assigned the role of housekeeper and cook in his after-school hours. "I know—and I knew then—that it wasn't her *fault* that my mother was sick. But still, I can't quite forgive her, or my father, for taking away my childhood. I just had to grow up too fast."

A woman who was the teen-aged eldest of five when her mother died was put in charge of the family. Her father was in no position to hire help, so she accepted the duties. "But believe me," she says, "I waited a long time to get married, and when I did, I told my husband I wanted nothing to do with children for a good while. It was ten years before I felt like being a mother again—and I think I am a worse one for having been forced into the role at too young an age."

Your children deserve their childhood. You can expect them to help out, but it isn't fair to saddle them with adult responsibilities too early. It isn't fair to you, either, to keep track of all the work and worries yourself. When the children of a news editor were having troubles, he had to take a lot of time off work, and he went about the office with a distracted frown because he'd been unable to find help.

Substitute mothers are hard to come by. Neighbors and visiting relatives can be a stopgap. Family service organizations and domestic employment agencies can provide experienced strangers to help with your house and children. Don't be afraid or too busy to screen and test these people thoroughly. They aren't just servants; they are mothering your kids, and you should pick them as carefully as you would a wife. The best solution—an excellent, warm, live-in housekeeper—is an expensive one. An aunt, grandmother, or sister who lives nearby or could come to stay is another answer, if you are lucky enough to have an extended, and willing, family.

If you have such a relative who would like to mother your children but can't leave a distant home for a long-term stay, you may have to consider moving yourself. A move immediately after a family crisis is not a good idea, and probably not a practical possibility. But if you can find a job and a home near a family helper, moving at the end of a school term may be better than having to endure a financial and personal strain just for the sake of staying put.

Pacing and Spacing

Some lucky single fathers have little trouble being the one consistent figure in their children's lives. Among those I've encountered, one is a writer who works at home, another is a doctor with an office in the house, and a third has his own small business, so he can set his own schedule around school hours.

If you have a standard full-time office or factory job, you face an added challenge in pacing yourself. If your job has required a lot of traveling, you may have to sacrifice advances and excitement for relocating in the home office. Most companies would be understanding about the special problems of single parents, and flexible about absences. If yours isn't, try finding an employer who does understand that your children deserve at least as much of your attention as he does.

But work isn't all your life. "Having Pete come to live with me sure cut down on my social life," writer Phil Stone said. Pete was 11 and moved in with Phil three years after the divorce. "I felt I had to be there every evening, and I certainly couldn't bring my dates home the way I used to. I gave up dating entirely for a while, until I found myself resenting Pete for messing up my love life."

Dating, fishing, golf, or barhopping with the guys—whatever away-from-home recreation a man enjoys, he shouldn't sacrifice because he's suddenly a "mother." At first, after a divorce or a death, it's true that your kids need your almost constant presence. But if you give up all your pleasures, you'll find yourself holding it against your children. Even mothers get time off, after all. A regular babysitter can fill in for you one or more evenings a week, or even for an entire weekend occasionally. During school vacations, a father would be wise to ship his kids off to grandma's or camp so that he can get back in touch with himself. Women are better mothers if they can untie their kids every now and then. The same applies to single dads.

Marrying Again?

If you do date, the time may come when you meet a woman you want to marry. She'll have to love you enough to take on your brood, too. And they and she should be given plenty of time to get to know each other. If your community standards permit, it is probably a good idea to have her live with all of you for a while before you make any final decision. In any case, you need lots of family time together before becoming a family.

Much as you love her, don't be surprised if your kids make her run the gauntlet. The steady girlfriend of a 7-year-old's father reports, "I got along all right with little Sam until I moved in with his father. Then the boy started snubbing me and hitting me. He would punch me in the breasts, and I couldn't stand for that. I couldn't figure out what I'd done wrong." She probably hadn't done anything wrong. But Sam's mother had "deserted" him when she left him in his father's care. Sam needed to take out his anger at his mother on the most convenient female. Hitting his father's girlfriend in the breast was his way of hurting all women—in a most symbolic fashion.

Single fathers report that their children take out hostility on *any* woman they see regularly—housekeeper, grandmother, or teacher. Whether they lost their mother through death or through divorce, they need to say, "My mother deserted me. She is a woman. You are a woman, and so I am angry at you." Add to this unconscious motivation the jealousy your kids may feel toward the woman who's taking some of your attention, and your girlfriend may be in for a rough time.

You can prepare her for it, and you can enforce rules to keep your kids from carrying their natural hostilities too far. Just don't take their initial hostility as a vote against the lady. On the other hand, it isn't a good idea to ask your children if you should marry her. Your personal life is not a matter for a family council. A friend says that when she was about 8, her father asked, "Would you like to have so-and-so for a new mother?" She told him, "No." He never remarried, and until she was grown she blamed herself for depriving him of a normal home life. Years later, it turned out that her father had meant the question casually, with no realistic intention of marrying the woman.

Marriage is an adult relationship and requires an adult decision. When you do remarry, the advice directed at stepfathers in the previous chapter applies to your kids' stepmother—only more so, because the emotions involved may be deeper and stronger.

Beyond Normal

Some hostility, some regression, some erratic behavior is normal after children lose their mother. You need to allow—even encourage—them to mourn and let out their grief and anger. Extra love, attention, and patience will help resolve most normal reactions. But where does "normal" stop?

Patty Christianson was only 4 when her mother died. A couple of weeks after the death, Patty displayed a disturbing reaction. She didn't cry, but she wouldn't eat, talk, or play. She wanted to do nothing but lie still all day, and when her father tried to activate her, he was alarmed to see that the girl could barely walk. The pediatrician and the specialists at the local hospital could find nothing physically wrong, but they warned Patty's father that

Single fathers have some unexpected challenges.

unless she started eating and living a more normal life, she would make herself sick. They recommended counseling at the mental health clinic.

After hearing Patty's story, a psychologist tried to get the girl to talk, or at least to act out through play whatever was bothering her. It didn't work, so the doctor used her intuition.

"You know, Patty, your Mommy didn't *want* to go away. She got so sick she couldn't live any more. But you didn't *make* her sick. All little girls get mad at their mothers sometimes. Sometimes, when they are angry, they say things like, 'I wish you would go away and never come back.' Sometimes, they just *think* those things. All children do. But thinking a bad thing about a person, wishing she would die, won't make her die. You didn't make your Mommy go away, even if you did think some bad thing about her."

Patty began to perk up. In subsequent visits to the psychologist, Patty's talk and play showed that the doctor's intuition had been right—the girl had been punishing herself for the mistaken idea that she had caused her mother's death. She had wished her dead, and the only just punishment for that was her own death. Once she was able to get these feelings out and realize that they were mistaken, she was ready to resume a normal life.

Children, almost from birth, are complex emotional and psychological networks. They can sense and feel all that an adult can, and more, but they haven't the experience to make rationality enter into their reactions. A child whose behavior is extreme, or who seems to be taking a long time to readjust after a crisis may harbor some problem that needs expert solutions. It isn't an expression of weakness or failure to seek help for your children—or for yourself.

Drawing the Line

Professional counseling for children, father, or both can help untangle some of the knots of worry from a father's gut. Many men, even after voluntarily giving up their wives, use their children as an "anchor," as the Eglesons put it. They need their kids for their own emotional stability in an upsetting period. Gradually, they make it a habit to turn toward their families. They become more of a mother than most mothers are—constantly supervising activities, brooding over minor problems or illnesses. They hang onto their children because they have nothing else. Obviously, such a situation is unhealthy for father and children. A man may need help to find his feet again so that he can let his children grow. Because kids, with or without mothers, need fathers.

Dan Sherman is one man who became such a good mother to his son that the boy lacked a father. Dan never got any housekeeping help after his wife left him, but did all the domestic chores himself, without asking his son to help. He never disciplined the boy, never insisted that he strive to do better at school, discouraged him from the masculine but injury-prone activities of other 12-year-olds. "I was afraid I'd turn him against me, or allow him to get hurt—and he was all I had." As a result, Dan's son grew up without any well-differentiated male-female model. In adolescence, he had trouble fitting in with either sex and almost stopped progressing altogether. Dan was finally persuaded to get help for his son and himself, but it was almost too late. Your children may need mothering, but they need fathering, too.

Enjoying

"I am very definitely my son's father," says Phil Stone. "I'm not his pal, and I'm not his mother . . . and I have never been happier since having him come to live with me." Once you figure out how to cope with the practicalities and have resolved the emotional conflicts, being a double-time father can be a most rewarding life. You have the opportunity to be involved with your children as most fathers never are.

But involvement, to be satisfying, requires knowledge. Most men aren't prepared for fatherhood, let alone motherhood.

"The only thing I knew about toilet training was that it had to get done sometime before the kid could go to school. I had no idea how or when."

"I read that a kid should have a balanced diet—but what the hell is a balanced diet?"

"And there I was, explaining menstruation to my daughter. And I hardly understood how my own body worked!"

Single fathers face some unexpected challenges. You may need a quick course in the care and feeding of children. A class at the Red Cross, hospital, college, or extension school might help, as would reading some of the books on child development listed in the appendix. Your female relatives and neighbors are probably more than willing to hand out advice.

And while you're asking about toilet training, nutrition, or menstruation, don't forget to ask, "How can I be a mother and a father and still have time to myself?" It's a hard question to answer, judging by the numbers of men who don't know how to be more than just a father and still have time for themselves.

14

Just a Father?

"When I was a boy, I used to do what my father wanted. Now I do what my boy wants. My problem is: when am I going to do what I want?"

Humorist Sam Levenson's problem is still with most men, though its cry has been muffled by the louder voices of women, asking, "When am I going to do what I want?"

In the late Sixties and early Seventies, we entered an antimale era. Men, and the male-oriented society that trained them, were blamed for forcing women into a position of second-class humanity. And let's face it, a lot of guys deserved the flak. Women got understandably tired of being treated as children or pretty playthings, of getting lower pay, of doing grubby work. They got tired of being the servant class in what sociologist Leonard Benson calls a "male-dominated, female-serviced" society.

"Being somebody's wife and somebody's mother means being nobody yourself." That isn't just a women's-lib catch phrase. As househusband John Michaels discovered, it can be a damned uncomfortable feeling, being shut up at home with a small child and being dependent on someone else, whom you must feed and clean up after, for money and contact with the outside world.

As somebody's wife and somebody's mother, I can tell you, that alone does not make up for being somebody myself.

So when my husband said, "In this book you're writing about fathers, I hope you're going to put in something about the problems fathers have," I was a bit bewildered.

"Well, I'm going to give you guys *credit* for bringing in the bread, playing with the kids, helping liberate women from some of the chores. Hopefully, the book will help some guys do it better. What more do you want?"

"How to put it? Like Mommy runs the house pretty much the way she wants to. If Daddy isn't the boss at work—and most men aren't—where does he get his satisfaction?"

I politely pooh-poohed and tut-tutted. "After all, bossing the house isn't exactly thrilling."

"Well, neither is working at most jobs—and a guy has to gratify his ego somehow. How's he going to do it and still take care of his wife and family?"

As is the case more often than I care to admit, he had a point.

Women envy men their greater freedom, their more exciting lives. But women who strive for more freedom by copying the lives of men are making a mistake. Men are trapped, too. A typical married man with kids is somebody's husband, somebody's father, *and* somebody's employee. He can't do what he wants any more than his wife can.

In a 1967 issue of *Parents' Magazine,* Hubert Humphrey praised the American father as a man who could balance his functions as breadwinner, role model, family man, and community member with the pursuit of his own individual happiness. And, wrote Humphrey, he is "holding up under the strain."

But is he? More alcoholics and drug addicts are men than women. Men commit five-sixths of the solved crimes in the country. Men are much more successful at suicide than women. Men fill the majority of beds in mental institutions. A man's life expectancy is some six years shorter than a woman's. Much as I may rankle at being treated "like a woman," faced with those statistics, I'd rather not be a man, thank you.

Then why have I written a book nagging men to be better fathers? Because in an age of feminine revolution, it is easy to forget that men are necessary for healthy kids. Because a lot of men deserve a pat on the back for sticking to fatherhood despite the flak. And because a good father can raise his kids, male or female, to be flexible enough to live in a society that is truly liberated.

To be that kind of father, a man first has to liberate himself. That doesn't mean that everyone should drop out of the rat race, though some may find that solution workable. Nor is it a call to all men to yield their roles to women, though that sometimes works, too. *It means finding the time to find yourself* and perhaps rearranging your life a little so that you, your wife, and your kids can reap more satisfaction than the pressures of your habitual roles allow. You may be stuck with being somebody's husband, somebody's father, and somebody's employee—but who are *you?*

Who Are You?

If you are like most men, you answer that question with a job description: "I'm a salesman, a steelworker, a teacher, a mechanic." If someone asked, "What is the most important thing in your life?" you would say, "My kids," if you are typical of the fathers I've talked with. It is as though we put blinders on a man, one labeled "career," the other marked "family." But there is a head between those blinders, and it is yours. What goes on inside it?

When you do get a chance to "do what *you* want," what is it that you will do? "I don't have time for that nonsense," you may snap. "And even if I did, I couldn't do anything about it."

"Look," the commuting father argues, "I get up before dawn to make the train for the city. My job? Well, it could be worse—I get to meet a variety of people, but it takes a lot of time, and it gets tedious after a while. It's dark when I get home, the kids are asleep or maybe, if I'm lucky, just

Who are you? A question you can ponder some night
when the TV is broken.

ready for bed. I have to hit the sack early to be ready for the alarm clock the next morning. I don't have time for my family, let alone myself."

"Self-fulfillment? What's that?" the factory-working father demands. "What I do all day you wouldn't even understand, because I'm not sure I do. But say it's like putting a bolt on a nut, one after the other—bolt, nut, bolt, nut. I don't even know if I have a self to fulfill any more. To the boss, I'm a machine. To my wife, I'm a paycheck. And the kids? Well, the kids think I'm okay, I guess, at least the younger ones. But all I really want out of them is to keep the noise down while I'm watching TV."

Every father has responsibilities to meet, and in an impersonal world it is hard to get much satisfaction out of meeting them. So it is all the more important to squeeze some of your own personal rewards out of the routine. When you were young, like Sam Levenson you did what your father wanted. But back then, what did you want to be when you were "grown up"?

Maybe you wanted to be an actor or a writer, but you found out (with a little help from your parents) that opportunities in those fields were small, and the pay was low. Or you hoped to be a scientist but couldn't face the schooling. Maybe you loved to work with your hands, but your parents scraped and saved so you could do something "better." Some guys wanted to work with their heads, but their parents couldn't afford the necessary education, so they work with their hands. Unless you are among the lucky few with a job that fits your skills and interests perfectly, with a comfortable home close to work, and with a secure future and plenty of free time, there is probably some secret self inside you that wants to be doing something you're not.

This yearning can spoil the good taste of the things you do enjoy. It can embitter you against your "fate," your wife and your kids. "If it weren't for them. . ." But it's not their fault. And everything you do doesn't have to be "for them." If everything you do is for someone else, you lose yourself. And that doesn't have to happen.

What would you rather be doing? What would you do with yourself if someone handed you enough money to keep you and your family secure forever? Most men don't know. And how much do you understand of the forces that got you where you are: your own childhood, your parents and their goals for you, your own needs and failings?

Who *are* you? It's not a foolish question. It is one you can ponder on the train, in the shower, or some night when the TV's broken. When you can answer it, you will know what the person inside you—who isn't somebody's father, somebody's husband, or somebody's employee—needs in order to get the most out of his life.

Is Your Family Worth Your Job?

"I never knew a man who didn't 'fulfill himself,' " a woman snorted at my concern for fathers' personal outlets. But that kind of comment assumes that the *escapes* from job pressures and tedium—drinking, TV-watching, golfing—are "self-fulfillment," or that a man's job is soul-satisfying. I don't think that this is the case for most men, and the mortality statistics would tend to confirm the opinion.

"American men make lousy fathers," Philip Wylie wrote, because they are too busy making good. Why? There's the money, the status, inflation, and the demand for luxury. There is also an element of insecurity—not financial, but personal. Men who unmercifully goad themselves toward one achievement after another, according to some psychologists, have a bad image of themselves. Often because of an unsatisfactory relationship with their own fathers, they have no sense of their own worth, and so continually need to prove themselves. As a result, they are home little, and when they do relate to their kids, they still have to defend their weak egos by never admitting error or allowing contradiction. Thus, their own kids grow up with a rotten self-image, and the cycle repeats.

Under the headline "High Price of Success," John Barnett reported in the *Wall Street Journal* that business pressures on the striving man lead to unhappy marriages, alcoholism, infidelity, child-beating, and emotionally disturbed children. Even if your condition is not

214

this critical, your job can take away more from your kids than your salary gives them. "Mandy *misses* her father so," a friend said. "For the last few months he's been working every night and every weekend. We have everything we need, but it's like he just can't stop making money."

A dimly remembered *New Yorker* cartoon sums up the problems of the overdriven father: "I don't know what Daddy does all day," says one kid to another, "but it makes him sick to his stomach."

You can cure the indigestion if you can straighten out your head, get your life in perspective. A little analysis, professional or self-, might help you realize that you're okay even if you aren't always out in front.

Do you have some ideal life-style in mind, fostered by the neighbors, advertisements, or your in-laws? Human wants are insatiable, as an economics professor once said. The ideal is always that, never real. If you are comfortable, if your family is fed and clothed, what is the point in killing yourself to add one luxury after another?

Maybe you feel that your wife demands a certain performance of you. If she actually is nagging you on to bigger and better things, you've got a marriage problem, not a job problem. Mike Sampson says that one reason for his divorce was his wife's demand that he forge ahead in a lucrative but boring career, when he wanted to sit back and take some time for himself. But you may be using your wife as an excuse. John Green struggled unhappily to become the perfect company man and then apologized to his wife, "Honey, I'm just not going to make it big in this business. I'm sorry, but I'm just not the type." She was surprised, because she'd never particularly wanted him to make the "big time," though she had never explicitly said, "Whatever you do, I like you."

Whoever is telling you to get ahead at all costs—whether it is yourself, your family, or your boss—is wrong.

The Mid-Thirties Crisis and Other Changes of Life

Take Oliver Wentworth, Jr. He's not a real person, but he is a type psychiatrists and other social scientists have

215

come to recognize. Ollie (his mother calls him Junior, but we'll call him Ollie) is 35. He has been married about twelve years and has three kids, the youngest of whom is 6. Ollie is an account executive for a large company in a big city. The pay is good, though lately it hasn't been keeping up too well with inflation. He can't let his family buy everything they want, but certainly they have all they need.

He commutes every day from a comfortable, if mortgaged, house with a filled two-car garage in a community with excellent schools. He and his wife, Angela, have had rough times in their marriage, like everyone, but things have settled down in the last four years and they get along pretty well. The American dream. All set.

Ollie had looked for a promotion last year, but the company brought in a new man instead. Ollie sat and figured: the way the ages were ranged in his office hierarchy, he'd be due for the sales-manager slot about the time his compulsory retirement came up. So he looked for another job, quietly, only to find that he was either too young or too old, too experienced or too inexperienced, for whatever was available. Oh well, he'll get his regular increases and his retirement benefits, so security is no worry. He likes his job all right, it's just that he has it licked and he's ready for a new challenge. But, better not rock any boats—the mortgage and car payments are still due like clockwork, there's college to think about, and his wife likes living where she does. So he tells himself things could be worse and sticks to the routine. Until one day. . .

Ollie is ripe for the "mid-thirties crisis." He has achieved what most men hope for—a good job, a stable family. But he has *done* it. He has solved the problems in his marriage and in his job, and he has nowhere else to go. Thirty-five is a long way from retirement, and the prospect of all that "happily ever after" can be demoralizing. Depending on Ollie's background and personality, he will (1) crack up, (2) go into a depression or "male malaise," or (3) run away with his secretary to start a "new life."

This syndrome has been dubbed the "mid-thirties crisis" because that is the earliest age when all the factors described first come together, leaving a man trapped, bored, and helpless.

Thirty-five is almost "old" in our youth-centered society. As a man like Ollie enters middle age, his difficulties only increase. While researching her *Wonderful Crisis of Middle Age,* Eda LeShan found to her surprise, that men have many more problems than women in facing middle age. They are "defensive and frightened," she says.

It is easy to see why. By his forties, a man may have achieved whatever "success" he's going to, and he may be disappointed. He may feel too old to switch careers, and besides, all those benefits tied up with his retirement plan or seniority system are too much to give up. He sees signs of aging, and that is anathema in our society. His kids have all but left home, and in the anticipation of life ahead of them have forgotten about the old man except when short of funds. Even his wife is getting older. So his psyche may indulge in a masculine change of life, complete with depression, sexual problems, and psychosomatic illnesses, and he may just happen to have a fatal car accident on the way to work one day.

Well, you *can* change your life without a "change-of-life." You can start a new career on the side, go back to school, move to a new part of the country if you're bored. Sure it might risk some of your "security," but that's better than risking your life.

If your routine seems purposeless, try adding purpose to change your perspective. You might volunteer to help some social service organization in your community—find some person or some group that needs *you.*

You might not even require a drastic shift. Insurance man John Green, pressured by the hard work and futility of his job, was ready to take up farming and free-lance anything. Instead, he found work at a different company and was able to relax. There *is* a middle ground between the mid-thirties crisis and dropping out, and it's worth looking for.

A while back, a New York magazine editor sought to escape the downhill race. He quit his job, left his wife, and fled to Pago-Pago (it's on the island of Tutuila, in the Pacific, and pronounced Pongo-Pongo, if you ever get the urge to buy a one-way ticket there). Reading the tale that he wrote of his experience, people realized that his problems flourished as well in Pago-Pago as they had in Manhattan.

As a friend who recently tried to escape urban pressures by moving to the country commented, "My paranoias went with me—they're very portable." Flight is not the answer to a dull or driven life. If your life revolves around two points—career and family—you'll lose your balance if one of those points gives way. It takes three points to determine a plane, in life as in geometry, and the third point is yourself.

Who Needs Pago-Pago?

Rather than take your paranoias to Pago-Pago, you'd do better to find yourself at home. And you can't find yourself in front of the TV or in a bottle of booze. Golfing weekends or week-long fishing trips may be fun, but the benefits are temporary. We all need to indulge ourselves in escape now and then, but amusement isn't satisfaction.

"Self-fulfillment," "self-actualization," "self-realization"—all are pop phrases coined to define a satisfaction that is lacking from much of contemporary life. Whatever you call it, you can use it if you're like most fathers I've observed. If you want to be more than "just" a father, you need to pursue an activity that makes you forget time, that leaves you feeling invigorated, or exhausted with a satisfied tiredness. You could pack the wife and kids into a sailboat and travel around the world. You could take up yoga or transcendental meditation. You could spend family weekends at sensitivity sessions or nudist camps. You *could,* but you don't have to in order to find that self between the blinders.

Hobbies aren't just games. Reading a book, or cooking lasagna, or building a bench, or painting a picture, or climbing a mountain offers you a means of getting to know yourself, of doing something that nobody else can do quite the same way. Some of the fathers I've talked with say that watching TV is their main recreation. Others have found ways to liberate themselves and their wives by flexing their schedules and habits a bit to make time for themselves.

Sam and Rachel Prince take turns. She likes to paint, and he's an amateur cabinetmaker. Monday and Wednesday evenings she's in charge of feeding, bathing, and bedding the kids, while he builds in his corner of the basement workshop. Tuesdays and Thursdays, he takes over upstairs, while she paints. Fridays, they usually loaf or go out. Over the weekend, Sam protects part of one day for her, and she sees that he isn't bothered part of the time. They have the rest of the weekend for chores or all-family activities.

The O'Rourkes have the same kind of arrangement, only they are both involved with community affairs and local politics. They do their best to schedule meetings that don't conflict. (When they do overlap, they take the kids along or hire a sitter.) It means that sometimes Bill has to make supper and mind the kids, but on other nights, he can go to his meetings without feeling guilty about leaving Kate alone with the kids.

Hank and Carla Jason don't always spend Hank's en-

Who needs Pago-Pago?

tire vacation together. He is a nature-lover and birdwatcher, and she's definitely not. So he often takes part of his time off in the wilds, and the rest with the family. In return, he guards the home front on weekends or holidays while Carla takes off with friends for shopping and theater sprees in the city.

It's easy to balance such switch-offs when both of you have some special interest to indulge. If it is only you who is looking for relief because your wife finds enough time for herself during the day, it is still possible. Jack Simmons wanted to go to graduate school, but he couldn't afford to quit his job, and night school seemed a drag. Luckily, he commutes into New York City, where a local university runs college and graduate classes on the commuter trains. Several times a week, he takes lecture classes in one car, and on the other trips he does his studying. In a few years, he'll have his degree, without taking any time off from his family. Meanwhile, he's keeping his mind alive on those long rides to and from work.

Maybe a college in your area would start a similar program on your transit system, with a little push from interested commuters. If not, you could sign up for early-morning, lunch-hour, or early-evening classes a few times a week. If you pitch in a little extra around the house, your wife won't miss you much in those few hours you aren't at home.

Of course, you don't have to be on your own to find yourself. You might be able to share your adventures with the family, as long as they really want to, and you're not trying to chip them off the old block. Teacher Walt Douglas does mountain climbing with his kids. Our Sean likes to spend time in the darkroom with his father, who now feels less guilty about disappearing in there on Saturdays. Tom Kelly, an accountant with an unfulfilled desire to be a baker, makes bread with his whole family. Joe Flaherty's kids seem to enjoy passing out petitions and campaign material for their dad's part-time politicking. The possibilities are almost endless. If you can combine your personal ambitions with your fathering time, you're doing something a father has always been for: passing on to the next generation his own enthusiasms, values, and knowledge.

Where do you get the extra energy? You may feel so flattened now by your daily got-to-make-ends-meet routine that you barely have the strength to open a can of beer and turn on the TV. But if you can make even a little time for your "want-to's," you'll have more stamina for all the "have-to's" in your life.

It's like jogging or any other strenuous exercise. You may be exhausted just thinking about it until your body gets used to it, but then you'll find you get *less* tired through the day. Just as jogging helps keep your heart and lungs working longer, so your hobbies—an old-fashioned term for "self-actualization"—keep your mind and spirit going. You aren't *just* a father, you are a person, too, and the more you give to yourself, the more you will have to give to your family.

15

Hear the Experts

Fourteen chapters on "What's a father for?" and do we have any good, solid answers? A few. Let's hear some more of what the experts have to tell us.

British psychologist B.D. Hendy: "Youngsters need from their fathers . . . love, compassion, understanding, protection but not overprotection, and an example of competence."

Dr. Allan Fromme in *The ABC of Child Care:* "What makes a good father? . . . If a man has a good personality to share with his children, he is a good father."

Eda LeShan in *How to Survive Parenthood:* "What children need from their father is for him to be himself— enjoying being a man, responding and reacting as the head of a household, passing on those traditions, values, and standards that he wants for his children, serving as a connecting link to the larger world, offering protection and guidance." The way Mrs. LeShan puts it, fathering sounds easy.

Dr. Benjamin Spock is concerned lest fathers have it *too* easy: "A common problem in America today is the father who is a great pal to his children and leaves all the disciplining to the mother. He may say that he doesn't want his children to resent him the way he sometimes resented his own father. He cheerfully ignores the little crises that arise all the time. . . . And when his wife begs him to take over some of the control . . . he does it too halfheartedly to have much effect. This reluctance of the father to be a disciplinarian is just as important a problem as that of the father who never plays with his children. It is part of a broader problem—the tendency in . . . certain . . . American families for the husband to act . . . like a son to his wife and for the wife to act like a mother to her husband.

"It isn't enough for a father to be a pal. Children . . . need to feel the strength of their father and to have a respect for him as an older, more authoritative person."

Louise Bates Ames of the Gesell Institute of Child Development told me that fathering comes naturally. "What's a father for?" she repeated. "This is certainly an East Coast, 1974 question. In other times and other places people would not have to ask this question—they KNOW what a father is for.

"Any good artwork, old or modern, which depicts the family group will tell you better than words can what the father's role is. He is the protector, the provider, the supporter. He is the one the rest of the family looks up to and depends on. He is an essential point in the father/mother/child triangle. Others can share the burden, but his is the responsibility.

"Some may argue that these are roles thrust upon him by a stereotyping Society. The biologist would answer that if you wiped out all Society's stereotypes and started the whole thing over again, you would end up with pretty much the same allocation of roles.

" . . . Perhaps a father's greatest contribution to his children is one he performs naturally, without too much thought. If behavior is a function of structure, as I believe to be the case, fathers and mothers, whatever their ideology, behave quite differently. And only a father, or at least a man in the household, can provide an adequate image for young girls and boys."

Not all experts on the subject have the professional status of an Ames or a Spock.

"What's a father for?" I asked Sean.

"A father is for children."

223

Right. So what do the kids have to say about their dads?

The ideal American father, according to 350 college students polled by Ralph Dreger and Anders Sweetland, is just, loving, controlled, lots of fun, clean, mild, demanding of high standards, and industrious—in that order.

A University of Illinois study found that the "ideal father" was moral, reputable, wholesome, calm, sociable, strong, decisive, independent, effective, wise, consistent, predictable, warm, and more strict than permissive.

Students in the University of Akron's course in fatherhood gathered these definitions:

"A father is someone who will eat a whole pretend meal from your doll dish."

"A father is someone who has his own special chair to relax in, when the dog isn't in it, and the ironing isn't over it."

"A father is someone who is still awake no matter what time your date brings you in."

Some four-year-olds I know answered my questions as follows:

"What's a father for, Lisa? What does your Daddy do for you?"

"He takes care of me, and plays with me. And he tells me not to do things."

"Does your Mommy do the same?"

"Yes, but she does them different."

"What's a father for, Jeff?"

"I don't know."

"How could I find out?"

"You can talk to my Daddy, and Lisa's, and Jenny's, and Anna's . . ."

"Well tell me, is it harder to be a Daddy, or a Mommy?"

"They're both the same harder."

Is there a difference between Mommy and Daddy? *Should* there be?

Dr. Ames adds: "A father's role is not and should not be that of a co-mother. In fact perhaps the most 'liberated' woman is she who can live her own personal and professional life with a fair degree of freedom but who can accept the fact that men's and women's responsibilities toward their children, and toward the family, differ greatly."

But Dr. Spock wrote me that fathers *should* share fully in child care.

Psychologist Robert Coles tends to go along with Spock. The function of a father, he has been quoted as saying, is "the same as the function of a mother. To give his children affection and support. To set standards. And, because it's usually the father with the outside job, to help the child learn about the outside world. But really, I don't think fathers should be very different from mothers."

Eda LeShan is adamant about the difference between parents. "It is marvelous that fathers are participating more with mothers, and staying home. But I'm still worried about the loss of a difference of functions. . . . Father's role really has to do with the *moral* education of kids . . . the moral bankruptcy of this country is due to father's failing in that role."

Is a father different from a mother? When I began this book, I thought I knew the answer. If Spock, LeShan, Coles, and Ames, professionals far more expert than I, give such apparently divergent responses, I suspect the answer may lie somewhere in the middle.

It's clear that fathering and mothering are both "harder"; that Mommy does the same things, "only different." Both fathers and mothers give love, protection, stimulation, and values to their children. Mother may win the bread, father may change the diapers, and yet—there are immutable differences. A mother, as the source of her children's life, is always going to be their comfort, their refuge for compassion. And a father, because he is the "first stranger" in his children's life, will always be a challenge, a judge to them, the one who urges them to strive to make the best of themselves.

I like the way Dr. Joyce Sullivan, who teaches the

University of Akron's course in fatherhood, sums up the question:

"The making of a father is a process which takes place over approximately two decades . . . the notion that the father's role is not as important as the mother's . . . is not only foolish, but dangerous in modern-day society.

"The process and eventual product of human liberation incorporates the vision that all of us—men and women, rich and poor, young and old—have the right, the responsibility and the freedom . . . to be what we think we can be, rather than the living example of some predetermined and assigned destiny through sex-role stereotyping.

"What is a father? He is a person who wants, feels, and cares. He is a person with a need to love his children and a need to be loved by his children. He is a person with a tremendous potential . . . "

What's a father for? There are no easy answers. You have to look into yourself, assess your own style of life. What are *you* comfortable with, no matter what tradition or faddism urges on you? *Your* goals, for *your*self and *your* children, are what count.

BIBLIOGRAPHY

Bibliography

SECTION I

Dickens, Charles. Comment quoted in Schwartz, Alvin. *To Be a Father.* New York: Crown Publishers, Inc., 1967.

Chapter One

Beadle, Muriel. "The Game of the Name," *The New York Times Magazine,* October 21, 1973, 38.

Benedek, Therese. "Fatherhood and Providing" in *Parenthood: Its Psychology and Psychopathology.* Edited by E. James Anthony and Therese Benedek, Boston: Little, Brown and Co., 1970.

Benson, Leonard. *Fatherhood: A Sociological Perspective.* New York: Random House, Inc., 1968.

Gilder, George F. "Sex and the Social Order," *The New Leader,* September 3, 1973, 5.

—————. *Sexual Suicide.* New York: Quadrangle Books, Inc.,1973

Goode, William J. (ed.). *The Contemporary American Family*. Chicago: Quadrangle Books, Inc., 1971.

Guttmacher, Alan F., M.D., et al. *Birth Control and Love*. New York: The Macmillan Co., 1969.

Hacker, Helen M. "New Burdens of Masculinity," *Marriage and Family Living*, August, 1957, 227.

Liebman, Sam (ed.). *Emotional Forces in the Family*. Philadelphia: J.B. Lippincott Co., 1959.

Nye, F. Ivan, and Bernardo, Felix M. *The Family: Its Structure and Interaction*. New York: The Macmillan Co., 1973.

Peck, Ellen. *The Baby Trap*. New York: Bernard Geis Assocs., 1971.

Pohlman, Edward. *The Psychology of Birth Planning*. Cambridge: Schenkman Publishing Co., Inc. 1969.

Terkel, Studs. " 'I Got No Use for Intellectuals, but I Want My Kid to Be an Effete Snob'," *New Times*, November 2, 1973, 48.

Chapter Two

Benson, Leonard. *Fatherhood*.

Bombeck, Erma. "When God Made a father," *Reader's Digest*, November, 1973, 187.

Coffin, Patricia. *One-Two-Three-Four-Five-Six: How to Enjoy the Years that Count*. New York: The Macmillan Co., 1972.

Goode, William J. *The Contemporary American Family*.

Hall, Carol. "It's All Right to Cry," from the album *Free to Be You and Me*. New York: Bell Records, 1972.

New York Times. March 16, 1969, p. 62, col. 3.

—————. September 4, 1972, p. 15, col. 3.

Scheinfeld, Amram. *Your Heredity and Environment*. Philadelphia: J. B. Lippincott Co., 1965.

Science Digest. March, 1966, 19.

Yankelovich, Daniel. Speech before the National Conference Board, October 19, 1973.

SECTION II

Biller, Henry B., and Weiss, Stephan D. "The Father-

Daughter Relationship and the Personality Development of the Female." *Journal of Genetic Psychology,* vol. 116 (1970), 79.

Chapter Three

Bachofen, Johann Jakob. *Myth, Religion, and Mother-right.* Princeton: Princeton University Press, 1967.

Benson, Leonard, *Fatherhood.*

Bohannon, Paul. *Social Anthropology.* New York: Holt, Rinehart and Winston, 1966.

Brenton, Myron. *The American Male.* New York: Coward, McCann, 1966.

Bubis, Gerald B. "The Modern Jewish Family," *Journal of Jewish Communal Service,* Spring, 1971.

The Cambridge Natural History. Codicote, England, 1968.

Daly, Mary. *Beyond God the Father.* Boston: Beacon Press, 1973.

Davis, Kingsley. "The Sociology of Parent-Youth Conflict," *American Sociological Review,* vol. 5 (1940), 523.

Erikson, Erik H. *Childhood and Society.* New York: W. W. Norton & Co., Inc., 1963.

Freud, Sigmund. *Totem and Taboo.* New York: W.W. Norton & Co., Inc., 1952.

Fuchs, Lawrence. *Family Matters.* New York: Random House, Inc., 1972.

Goldberg, Steven. *The Inevitability of Patriarchy.* New York: William Morrow and Co., 1973.

Goode, William. *The Contemporary American Family.*

Gough, Kathleen. "The Origin of the Family," *Journal of Marriage and Family Living,* November, 1971.

Henry, Jules. *Culture Against Man.* New York: Random House, Inc., 1963.

Herskovits, Melville J. *Man and His Works.* New York: Alfred A. Knopf, Inc., 1949.

Hockett, Charles F., and Ascher, Robert. "The Human Revolution," *Current Anthropology,* vol. 5 (1964), 135.

Kenkel, William F. *The Family in Perspective.* New York: Appleton-Century-Crofts, 1973.

LaBarre, Weston. *The Human Animal.* Chicago: University of Chicago Press, 1954.

Leakey, L. S. B. *Adam's Ancestors*. New York: Harper & Row Publishers, Inc., 1960.

Lowie, Robert H. *Social Organization*. New York: Rinehart & Co., 1956.

Malinowski, Bronislaw. *Sex and Repression in Savage Society*. New York: Harcourt, Brace and World, 1927.

——————. *The Father in Primitive Society*. W.W. Norton & Co., 1927.

Mead, Margaret. *Male and Female*. New York: Dell Publishing Co., 1973.

Milne, Lorus, and Milne, Margery. *The Nature of Life*. New York: Crown Publishers, 1970.

Nye, F. Ivan, Bernardo, Felix M. *The Family*.

Parsons, Talcott. "The Father Symbol: An Appraisal in the Light of Psychoanalytic and Sociological Theory," in Bryson, Lyman *et al*. (eds.)., *Symbols and Values*. New York: Harper & Row, 1954.

——————, Bales, Robert *et al*. *Family, Socialization, and Interaction Process*. New York: Free Press, 1955.

Pfeiffer, John E. *The Emergence of Man*. New York: Harper & Row Publishers, Inc., 1969.

Shideler, Mary McD. "The Father and the Fathers," *Christian Century*, August 13, 1969, 1061.

Washburn, Sherwood L. (ed.). *Social Life of Early Man*. New York: Wenner-Gren Foundation, 1961.

——————. "Speculations on the Interrelations of the History of Tools and Biological Evolution," *Human Biology*, vol. 31 (1959), 21.

Wendt, Herbert. *From Ape to Adam*. New York: The Bobbs-Merrill Co., Inc., 1972.

Whiting, John W. M., and Child, Irvin L. *Child Training and Personality*. New Haven: Yale University Press, 1953.

Chapter Four

Ames, Louise Bates. Personal interview with author. Nov. 6, 1973.

Barclay, Dorothy. "The Men in Children's Lives," *New York Times Magazine*, June 19, 1955, 38.

Benedek, Therese. "Fatherhood and Providing."

Benson, Leonard. *Fatherhood*.

Biller, Henry B. *Father, Child, and Sex Role*. Lexington, Mass.: Heath-Lexington Books, 1971.

Blood, Robert O. *The Family*. New York: Free Press, 1972.

Burton, Roger V., and Whiting, John W. M. "The Absent Father and Cross-Sex Identification," *Merrill-Palmer Quarterly*, vol. 7 (1961), 85.

Child Study Association. "The Man in the Family," *Child Study*, Summer 1957.

Collins, Cyrus. "What Children Need from a Father," *Parents' Magazine*, June, 1956, 44.

English, O. Spurgeon, M.D. "The Psychological Role of the Father in the Family," *Social Casework*, vol. 35 (1954), 323.

——————, and Foster, Constance J. *Fathers Are Parents, Too*. New York: G. P. Putman's Sons 1951.

"Exploring Childhood," Educational Development Center, 1972.

Family Service Association of America. *The Significance of the Father*. Washington, D. C., April 1959.

Fraiberg, Selma. *The Magic Years*. New York: Charles Scribner's Sons, 1959.

Fuchs, Lawrence. *Family Matters*.

Ginott, Haim. *Between Parent and Child*. New York: Avon Books, 1969.

Greenstein, Jules M. "Father Characteristics and Sextyping," *Journal of Personality and Social Psychology*, vol. 3. (1966), 271.

Handel, Gerald. "Sociological Aspects of Parenthood," in Anthony, E. James, and Benedek, Therese (eds.), *Parenthood: Its Psychology and Psychopathology*.

Herzog, Elizabeth, and Sudia, Cecilia E. "Boys in Fatherless Families," U. S. Department of Health, Education, and Welfare, Children's Bureau, 1970.

——————. "Fatherless Homes: A Review of Research," *Children*, vol.15 (1968), 177.

Hochstein, Rollie. "An Interview with Child Psychologist Robert Coles," *Family Circle*, November, 1973, 76.

Homan, William E., M.D. *Child Sense*. New York: Bantam Books, 1970.

Kramer, Rita. "For Parent Effectiveness—On-the-job Training," *New York Times Magazine*, March 28, 1971, 102.

Kruger, W. Stanley. "Teaching Parenthood," *American Education*, December, 1972.

Kulkin, Mary Ellen. Tape-recorded interviews with fathers, 1973.

LeMasters, E. E. *Parents in Modern America*. Homewood, Illinois: Dorsey Press, 1970.

Leonard, Marjorie H. "When Fathers Drop Out," *New York Times Magazine*, April 20, 1969, 81.

LeShan, Eda. *How to Survive Parenthood*. New York: Random House, Inc., 1965.

Levine, Milton I., M.D., and Seligman, Jean H. *The Parents' Encyclopedia*, New York: Thomas Y. Crowell Co.,1973.

Life Magazine. "The New Fathers," July 14, 1972.

Montagu, Ashley. "Every Day Is Father's Day, *Parents' Magazine*, June, 1965, 43.

New York Times. January 13, 1954, p. 54, col. 3.

—————. September 2, 1960, p. 25, col. 5.

—————. July 24, 1972, p. 18, col. 4.

—————. March 21, 1973, p. 45, col. 3.

—————. November 5, 1973, p. 55, col. 5.

Nichols, Robert C. "Factor Analysis of Parental Attitudes of Fathers," *Child Development*, vol. 33 (1962), 791.

Ostrovsky, Everett S. *Father to the Child*. New York: G. P. Putnam's Sons, 1959.

Papanek, Miriam L. "Authority and Sex Roles in the Family," *Journal of Marriage and the Family*, vol. 31 (1969), 88.

Santrock, John W. "Paternal Absence, Sex Typing, and Identity," *Developmental Psychology*, vol. 2 (1970), 264.

Shannon, William V. "What Code of Values Can We Teach Our Children Now?" *New York Times Magazine*, January 16, 1972, 9.

Stapelton, Constance. "Teaching Children to Be Parents," *Parade*, March 11, 1973.

Sutton-Smith, Brian, Rosenberg, B.G., and Landy, Frank. "Father-Absence Effects in Families of Different Sibling Composition," *Child Development*, vol. 39 (1968), 1213.

Swartz, Jon D. Review of *Father, Child and Sex Role*, in

Journal of Marriage and the Family, vol. 35 (1973), 558.

Tasch, Ruth J. "Interpersonal Perceptions of Fathers and Mothers," *Journal of Genetic Psychology,* vol. 87 (1955), 59.

Thomas, Gordon, M.D. *Parent-Effectiveness Training.* New York: Peter H. Wyden, Inc., 1970.

Thomas, Mary M. "Children with Absent Fathers," *Journal of Marriage and the Family,* vol. 30 (1968), 88.

U.S. Department of Health, Education, and Welfare, Children's Bureau. "Education for Parenthood," *Children Today,* March 4, 1973.

Winter, Ruth. "Psychologists Sound Off on What Makes a Good Father," *Science Digest,* June, 1973, 14.

Withers, Samuel. "The 364 Other Days with Father," *New York Times Magazine,* June 16, 1963, 56.

Yarro, Marion Radke. "Problems of Methods in Parent-Child Research," in Medinnus, Gene R. (ed.), *Readings in the Psychology of Parent-Child Relations.* John Wiley and Sons, 1967.

Yarrow, Leon J. "Separation from Parents During Early Childhood," in Hoffman, L. W. and M. L. (eds.), *Review of Child Development Research.* New York: Russell Sage, 1964.

Zolotow, Charlotte. *William's Doll.* New York: Harper & Row publishers, Inc., 1972.

Chapter Five

Benson, Leonard. *Fatherhood.*

Biller, Henry B. *Father, Child, and Sex Role.*

—————, and Weiss, Stephan D. "The Father-Daughter Relationship and the Personality Development of the Female."

Blood, Robert O. *The Family.*

Bronfenbrenner, Urie. "Freudian Theories of Identification and Their Derivatives," *Child Development,* vol. 31 (1960), 15.

Dodson, Fitzhugh, M.D. *How to Parent.* New York: New American Library, 1971.

English, O. Spurgeon, M.D., and Foster, Constance J. *Fathers are Parents, Too.*

"Father-daughter Relations in School Phobia," *Smith College Studies in Social Work*, 1961, 31.

Forrest, Tess. "Paternal Roots of Male Character Development," *Psychoanalytic Review*, vol. 54 (1967), 81.

Fraiberg, Selma. *The Magic Years*.

Friedrich, Otto. "Reflections in a Father's Eye," *Esquire*, July, 1973, 116.

Hetherington, E. Mavis. "Girls Without Fathers," *Psychology Today*, February, 1973, 46.

Homan, William E., M. D. *Child Sense*.

Klein, Ted. *The Father's Book*. New York: William Morrow & Co., Inc. 1968.

Leonard, Marjorie. "When Fathers Drop Out."

LeShan, Eda. *Natural Parenthood*. New York: Signet Books, 1970.

Lipman-Blumen, Jean. "How Ideology Shapes Women's Lives," *Scientific American*, March, 1972, 34.

Rothbart, Mary K., and Maccoby, Eleanor. "Parents' Differential Reactions to Sons and Daughters," *Journal of Personality and Social Psychology*, vol. 4 (1966), 237.

Spock, Benjamin, M.D. Letter to author, December 11, 1973.

Sutton-Smith, Brian, *et al*. "Father-Absence Effects..."

Thomas, Mary M. "Children With Absent Fathers."

Chapter Six

Barclay, A., and Cusumano, D. "Father-Absence, Cross-Sex Identity and Field-Dependent Behavior in Male Adolescents," *Child Development*, vol. 38 (1967), 243.

Benedek, Therese. "Fatherhood and Providing."

Benson, Leonard. *Fatherhood*.

Biller, Henry B. "Father Absence and Masculine Development in Lower-class Negro and White boys," *Child Development*, vol. 39 (1968), 1003.

—————. "Father-absence, Maternal Encouragement, and Sex-role Development in Kindergarten-age Boys," *Child Development*, vol. 40 (1969), 639.

—————. *Father, Child, and Sex Role*.

Bronfenbrenner, Urie. "Freudian Theories of Identification . . ."

Dodson, Fitzhugh, M. D. *How To Parent.*

Forrest, Tess. "Paternal Roots of Male Character Development."

Fraiberg, Selma. *The Magic Years.*

Greenstein, Jules M. "Father Characteristics and Sex-Typing."

Herzog, Elizabeth, and Sudia, Cecelia E. "Boys in Fatherless Families."

Hetherington, E. Mavis. "Effects of Paternal Absence on Sex-Typed Behaviors in Negro and White Pre-Adolescent Males," *Journal of Personality and Social Psychology,* vol. 4 (1966), 87.

Homan, William E., M.D., *Child Sense.*

Journal of Abnormal and Social Psychology. Vol. 64 (1962), 361.

Klein, Ted. *The Father's Book.*

Marmor, Judd, M.D. *Sexual Inversion: The Multiple Roots of Homosexuality.* New York: Basic Books, 1968.

Mead, Margaret. "The Job of the Children's Mother's Husband," in Goode, William J., *The Contemporary American Family.*

New York Times. February 10, 1971, p. 48, col. 1.

"Preventing Homosexuality," *Family Life,* vol. 31 (1971), 1.

Spock, Benjamin, M.D. *Baby and Child Care.* New York: Pocket Books, 1974.

Thompson, George G. *Child Psychology.* Boston: Houghton Mifflin Co., 1962.

Wyden, Peter and Barbara. "Growing Up Straight—the Father's Role," *New York Times Magazine,* May 26, 1968, 69.

Chapter Seven

Albrecht, Margaret. *The Complete Guide for the Working Mother.* Award Books, 1970.

Aldous, Joan. "Children's Perceptions of Adult Role Assumption," *Journal of Marriage and the Family,* vol. 34 (1972), 55.

—————. "Wives' Employment Status and Lower-class Men as Husband-Fathers: Support for the Moynahan Thesis," *Marriage and Family Living*, vol. 31 (1969), 469.

Ames, Louise Bates. Personal interview with the author, Nov. 6, 1973.

Beels, C. Christian. "Whatever Happened to Father?" *New York Times Magazine*, August 25,1974, 10.

Benson, Leonard. *Fatherhood.*

Blood, Robert O. *The Family.*

Bott, Elizabeth. *Family and Social Network.* London: Tavistock Publishers, 1957.

Brenton, Myron. *The American Male.*

Callahan, Sidney C. *The Working Mother.* New York: The Macmillan Co., 1971.

Chilman, C. William. "If I Had Another Chance at Fatherhood," *Today's Health,* April 1969, 56.

Coffin, Patricia. *One-Two-Three-Four-Five-Six.*

Cotton, Dorothy Whyte. *The Case for the Working Mother.* New York: Stein and Day, 1965.

Ehrlich, Phyllis. "Father in the Family Circle," *New York Times Magazine,* June 12, 1960, 65.

Foster, June E. "Father Images: Television and Ideal," *Journal of Marriage and the Family,* vol.26 (1964), 353.

Freud, Sigmund. *Totem and Taboo.*

Friedan, Betty. *The Feminine Mystique.* New York: W. W. Norton & Co., 1963.

Fuchs, Lawrence. *Family Matters.*

Gould, Robert. "Husbands Talk About Liberated Wives," *New York Times Magazine,* June 18, 1972, 11.

Hartley, Ruth E. "Children's Perceptions of Sex Preference in Four Cultural Groups," *Journal of Marriage and the Family,* vol. 31 (1969), 380.

Hoover, Mary B. *The Responsive Parent.* New York: Parents' Magazine Press, 1972.

Kulkin, Mary Ellen. Taped interviews with fathers.

Landau, Genevieve M. "Changing Role of American Parents," *Parents' Magazine,* May, 1973.

LeShan, Eda. Telephone interview with the author, October 18, 1973.

Levin, Phyllis Lee. "Putting Down Father," *New York Times Magazine,* March 21, 1965, 79.

Lloyd-Jones, Jenkin. "Let's Bring Back Dad," *Vital Speeches,* May 15, 1973, 473.

Lowie, Robert. *Social Organization.*

Lyttle-Holmston, Lynda. *The Two-Career Family.* Cambridge: Schenckman Publishing Co., 1972.

Mead, Margaret. "The Job of the Children's Mother's Husband."

Mogey, John M. "A Century of Declining Paternal Authority," *Marriage and Family Living,* vol. 19 (1957), 234.

New York Times. August 11, 1970, p. 32, col. 5.

——————. May 27, 1972, p. 14, col. 1.

——————. November 11, 1972, p. 42, col. 1.

——————. January 6, 1973, p. 1, col. 7.

——————. October 13, 1973, p. 30, col. 1.

——————. October 16, 1973, p. 38, col. 1.

Nye, F. Ivan, and Bernardo, Felix M. *The Family.*

Otto, Herbert (ed.). *Family in Search of a Future.* New York: Appleton-Century-Crofts, 1970.

Papanek, Miriam L. "Authority and Sex Roles in the Family."

Ridley, Carl S. "Exploring the Impact of Work Satisfaction and Involvement in Marriage Interaction," *Journal of Marriage and the Family,* vol 35 (1973), 229.

Spock, Benjamin, M.D. Letter to author.

Toffler, Alvin. *Future Shock.* New York: Random House, Inc., 1970.

U.S. Department of Commerce, Bureau of the Census. *General Social and Economic Characteristics, 1970 Census of Population.* Washington, D.C., June, 1972.

——————. *Statistical Abstract of the United States.* Washington, D.C., 1971.

——————. *We, the American Women.* Washington, D.C., March, 1973.

Withers, Samuel. "The 364 Other Days with Father."

Wylie, Philip. *Generation of Vipers.* New York: Holt, Rinehart and Winston, 1942.

SECTION III

Felsen, Henry Gregor. *Letters to a Teen-age Son.* New York: Dodd, Mead & Co., Inc., 1962.

Chapter Eight

Ames, Louise Bates, Interview, Nov. 6, 1973.

Benson, Leonard. *Fatherhood.*

Biller, Henry B. *Father, Child, and Sex Role.*

Boston Children's Hospital Medical Center. *Accident Handbook.* New York: Dell Publishing Co., 1966.

Bowlby, John. *Attachment and Loss:* Vol. 1, *Attachment.* New York, Basic Books, 1969.

Cook, Joan. "Reducing Risks for Expectant Fathers," *New York Times Magazine,* July 5, 1964, 19.

English, O. Spurgeon, M.D., and Foster, Constance. J. *Fathers Are Parents, Too.*

Erikson, Erik H. *Childhood and Society.*

"Fathers Wanted!" *Family Life,* vol. 33 (1973),1.

Forrest, Tess. "Paternal Roots of Male Character Development."

Fraiberg, Selma, *The Magic Years.*

Gesell, Arnold, M.D., and Ilg, Frances, M.D. *Infant and Child in the Culture of Today.* New York: Harper & Row Publishers, Inc., 1943.

Gilbreth, Frank B., Jr. *How To Be a Father.* New York: Thomas Y. Crowell Co., 1958.

Hetherington, E. Mavis. "Effects of Paternal Absence on Sex-Typed Behaviors in Negro and White Pre-Adolescent Males."

Hotchner, A. E. *Papa Hemingway.* New York: Random House, Inc., 1966.

LeMasters, E. E. "Parenthood as Crisis," *Journal of Marriage and the Family,* vol. 19 (1957), 352.

Life Magazine, "The New Fathers."

Neisser, Edith G. *Primer for Parents of Preschoolers.* New York: Parents' Magazine Press, 1972.

—————, and Neisser, Walter. "Making the Grade as Dad," Public Affairs Committee.

New York Times, January 6, 1973. p. 1, col. 7.

Olofson, Shirley. "On the Vagaries of Child-Care Books," *American Libraries,* December, 1970, 1036.

Schaefer, George, M.D. *Expectant Father.* New York: Barnes and Noble, 1972.

Spock, Benjamin, M.D. *Baby and Child Care.*

——————. Letter, December 11, 1973.

Stone, L. Joseph, and Church, Joseph. *Childhood and Adolescence.* New York: Random House, Inc. 1968.

Szasz, Suzanne. "Father Takes a Turn," *Parents' Magazine,* April 1972.

Thoms, Rachele. "The Challenge of Fatherhood," *Parents' Magazine,* June, 1967, 41.

United States Department of Health, Education, and Welfare, Children's Bureau. *Infant Care.* Washington, D.C.: Government Printing Office, 1966.

Weeks, Louis. "Father Takes Care of the Baby," *Parents' Magazine,* February, 1971, 60.

Chapter Nine

Benson, Leonard. *Fatherhood.*

Dodson, Fitzhugh, M.D. *How to Parent.*

English, O. Spurgeon, M.D., and Foster, Constance J. *Fathers Are Parents, Too.*

Gesell, Arnold, M.D., and Ilg, Frances, M.D. *The Child from Five to Ten.* New York: Harper & Row Publishers, Inc., 1946.

——————, and Ames, Louise Bates. *Youth: The Years from Ten to Sixteen.* New York: Harper & Row Publishers, Inc., 1956.

Ginott, Haim. *Between Parent and Child.*

Gosse, Edmund. *Father and Son.* New York: Charles Scribner's Sons, 1907.

Hayakawa, S. I. "The Most Precious Gift a Father Can Give His Son," *Today's Health,* June, 1971, 21.

Liebman, Sam (ed.). *Emotional Forces in the Family.*

Kramer, Rita. "For Parent Effectiveness . . . "

Mogal, Doris P. *Character in the Making.* New York: Parents' Magazine Press, 1972.

Neisser, Edith G. and Walter. "Making the Grade as Dad."

New York Times, January 6, 1973.

Spock, Benjamin, M.D. *Baby and Child Care*.

————. Letter, December 11,1973.

Stone, L. Joseph, and Church, Joseph. *Childhood and Adolescence*.

Time Magazine. "On Being an American Parent," December 15, 1967, 30.

Chapter Ten

Albrecht, Margaret. *Parents and Teenagers: Getting Through to Each Other*. New York: Parents' Magazine Press, 1972.

Ames, Louise Bates. Interview, November 6, 1973.

Arnstein, Helene, *Getting Along with Your Grown-Up Children*. Philadelphia: Evans, 1970.

Benson, Leonard. *Fatherhood*.

Dodson, Fitzhugh, M.D. *How to Parent*.

Erikson, Erik H. *Childhood and Society*.

Forrest, Tess. "Paternal Roots of Male Character Development."

Gesell, Arnold, M.D., Ilg, Frances, M.D., and Ames, Louise Bates. *Youth: The Years from Ten to Sixteen*.

Hochstein, Rollie. "An Interview with Child Psychologist Robert Coles," *Family Circle*, November, 1973, 76.

Jones, Eve. *Intelligent Parent's Guide to Raising Children*. New York: Collier Books, 1961.

Lawrence, Joan. "The Man in Her Life," *New York Times Magazine*, August 15, 1965, 52.

Leonard, Marjorie H. "When Fathers Drop Out."

Minton, Lynn. *Growing into Adolescence*. New York: Parents' Magazine Press, 1972.

Neisser, Edith and Walter. "Making the Grade as Dad."

Payne, Donald E., and Mussen, Paul H. "Father-identification Among Adolescent Boys." *Journal of Abnormal and Social Psychology*, vol. 52. (1956), 338.

Stone, L. Joseph, and Church, Joseph. *Childhood and Adolescence*.

Chapter Eleven

Arnstein, Helene. *Getting Along with Your Grown-Up Children.*

Curtin, Sharon. *Nobody Ever Died of Old Age.* Boston: Atlantic Monthly Press, 1973.

De Beauvoir, Simone. *The Coming of Age.* New York: G.P. Putnam's Sons, 1972.

Erikson, Erik H. *Childhood and Society.*

Hurwitz, Ken. "My Thanks to My Parents for Offering Me Their Dreams," *New Times,* October 19, 1973, 87.

Irving, Howard H. "Relations Between Married Couples and Their Parents," *Social Casework,* vol. 52 (1971), 91.

Johnson, Sheila K. "Three Generations—One Household," *New York Times Magazine,* August 19, 1973, 24.

Klein, Ted. *The Father's Book.*

New York Times. June 12, 1971, p. 29, col. 4.

——————. December 31, 1972, X p. 1.

——————. May 1, 1973, p. 22, col. 1.

Chapter Twelve

Beatman, Frances J. "When a Child Gets a New 'Parent'," *New York Times Magazine,* January 29, 1961, 49.

Benson, Leonard. *Fatherhood.*

Biller, Henry B. "Father-absence, Maternal Encouragement, and Sex-role Development in Kindergarten-age Boys."

——————, and Weiss, Stephan D. "The Father-Daughter Relationship and the Personality Development of the Female."

Despert, J. Louise, M.D. *Children of Divorce.* New York: Doubleday & Co., Inc., 1953.

——————. "The Children of Emotional Divorce," *New York Times Magazine,* November 27, 1960, 103.

Eberhart, E. T. "Fathers Without Children," *Parents' Magazine,* April, 1965, 66.

Egleson, Jim, and Egleson, Janet Frank. *Parents Without Partners*. New York: E. P. Dutton & Co., Inc. 1961.

Gaylord, C. L. "Something Is Loose in the Marital Woods," *ABA Journal,* vol. 59 (1973), 1306.

Gold, Herbert. *Love and Like*. New York: The Dial Press, 1960.

Herzog, Elizabeth, and Sudia, Cecelia E. "Fatherless Homes: A Review of Research."

Hetherington, E. Mavis. "Girls Without Fathers."

Hunt, Morton L. *The World of the Formerly Married*. New York: McGraw-Hill, Inc.,1966.

Jones, Eve. *Raising Your Child in a Fatherless Home*. New York: The Free Press, 1963.

Klein, Ted. *The Father's Book*.

LeShan, Eda. Telephone interview, October 18, 1973.

Life Magazine. "The American Family—How It's Changed," December 16, 1966, 4.

Lobsenz, Norman. "A Second Chance at Fatherhood," *Parents' Magazine,* June, 1972, 34.

New York Times. December 25, 1963, p. 29, col. 2.

——————. February 17, 1967, p. 43, col. 1.

——————. June 2, 1969, p. 50, col. 1.

——————. November 14, 1969, p. 73, col. 1.

——————. March 7, 1973, p. 48, col. 1.

"The Role of the Father," *Journal of Parents Without Partners,* March, 1962.

Schlesinger, Benjamin. "The One-Parent Family: An Overview," *Family Life Coordinator,* vol. 15 (1966), 133.

Thomson, Helen. *The Successful Stepparent*. New York: Harper & Row Publishers, Inc., 1966.

Withers, Samuel. "Some Guide Rules for Divorced Fathers," *New York Times Magazine,* September 29, 1963, 103.

——————. "The 364 Other Days with Father.

Wolf, Anna W. M., and Stein, Lucille. "The One-Parent Family," New York: Public Affairs Committee, 1973.

Chapter Thirteen

Barclay, Dorothy. "The One-Parent Family," *New York Times Magazine,* January 26, 1958, 46.

Bowlby, John. *Attachment and Loss:* Vol. 2, *Separation: Anxiety and Anger.* New York: Basic Books, 1973.

Egleson, Jim, and Egleson, Janet Frank. *Parents Without Partners.*

Klein, Carole. *The Single Parent Experience.* New York: Walker Publishing Co., Inc., 1973.

Koch, Joanne. "Let's Be More Just in Child-Custody Decisions," *Today's Health,* November, 1972, 68.

New York Times, June 30, 1972, p. 30, col. 1.

—————. November 12, 1973, p. 42, col. 1.

—————. January 28, 1973, IV, p. 12, col. 3.

—————. February 16, 1973, p. 44, col. 3.

Schlesinger, Benjamin. "The One-Parent Family: An Overview."

Withers, Samuel. "The 364 Other Days with Father."

Wolf, Anna W. M. *Helping Your Child Understand Death.* New York: Child Study Association, 1973.

————— and Stein, Lucille. "The One-Parent Family."

Chapter Fourteen

Barclay, Dorothy. "How to Live with Father's Job," *New York Times Magazine,* July 23, 1961, 48.

Barnett, John. "The High Price of Success," *Science Digest,* October, 1967, 26 (reprinted from *Wall Street Journal*).

Benson, Leonard. *Fatherhood.*

Birdwhistle, Ray L. "The Idealized Model of the American Family," *Social Casework,* April, 1970, 195.

Bowley, Mary A. Letter. *Atlantic Monthly,* September, 1973, 39.

Brenton, Myron. *The American Male.*

Chilman, C. William. "If I Had Another Chance at Fatherhood."

Fuchs, Lawrence. *Family Matters.*

Hacker, Helen M. "The New Burdens of Masculinity."

Hoover, Mary B. *The Responsive Parent.*

Humphrey, Hubert H. *Parents' Magazine,* June, 1967, 36.

LeShan, Eda. Telephone interview, October 18, 1973.

—————. *The Wonderful Crisis of Middle Age.* New York: David McKay Co., Inc.,1973.

Levenson, Sam. Comment quoted in Schwartz, Alvin. *To Be a Father.*

Messer, Alfred K. "The Self-Made Man as Father," *New York Times Magazine,* March 19, 1967, 123.

New York Times. December 31, 1972, p. 1.

—————. September 24, 1973, p. 33, col. 3.

—————. November 11, 1973, p. 41, col. 5.

O'Gara, James. "Oh Dad, Poor Dad," *Commonweal,* October 12, 1962, 64.

Time Magazine. "The American Family: Future Uncertain," December 28, 1972, p. 34.

U.S. Dept. of Commerce. *Statistical Abstract,* 1971.

Velie, Leslie. "Where Have All the Fathers Gone?" *Reader's Digest,* April, 1973, 155.

Wylie, Philip. "American Men Are Lousy Fathers," *Reader's Digest,* March, 1956, 99.

Chapter Fifteen

Ames, Louise Bates. Personal letter to the author, November 22, 1973.

Barclay, Dorothy. "The Men in Children's Lives," *New York Times Magazine,* June 19, 1955, 38 (quoting B. D. Hendy).

Dreger, Ralph M., and Sweetland, Anders. *Journal of Genetic Psychology,* vol. 96 (1960), 115.

Fromme, Allan, M.D. *The ABC of Child Care.* Pocket Books, 1969.

Hochstein, Rollie. "An Interview with Child Psychologist Robert Coles."

LeShan, Eda. Telephone interview, Oct. 18, 1973.

LeShan, Eda. *How to Survive Parenthood.*

Levin, Phyllis Lee. "Putting Down Father."

Spock, Benjamin. Letter, December 11, 1973.

Sullivan, Joyce. Personal letter to author, December 13, 1973.

For Further Help and Information

American Association of Marriage and Family Counselors
225 Yale Avenue
Claremont, California 91711
Standard-setter for the profession; referral service.

Association for Childhood Education International
3615 Wisconsin Avenue, N.W.
Washington, D.C. 20016
Source for lists of recommended reading for children and adults, and other information on early childhood.

Child Study Association of America—Wel-Met, Inc.
50 Madison Avenue
New York, N.Y. 10010
Source for pamphlets, reading lists, and other information on child-rearing and family life.

The Children's Book Council, Inc.
175 Fifth Avenue
New York, N.Y. 10010

Source for suggestions on children's books about specific and general topics.

Family Service Association of America
44 East 23d Street
New York, N.Y. 10010

Standard-setter for a variety of local social-service agencies; source of information on family problems.

Maternity Center Association
48 East 92d Street
New York, N.Y. 10028

Source for information on pregnancy and childbirth.

National Association for Mental Health
1800 North Kent Street
Rosslyn, Virginia 22209

Source for information on local agencies involved in the prevention and treatment of mental illness.

Parents Without Partners, Inc.
7910 Woodmont Avenue
Washington, D.C. 20014

Organization for single, widowed, and divorced parents; local chapters throughout U.S. and Canada.

Planned Parenthood Federation of America, Inc.
810 Seventh Avenue
New York, N.Y. 10019

Source for information on birth control and fertility problems.

Public Affairs Committee, Inc.
381 Park Avenue South
New York, N.Y. 10016

Publishes informative pamphlets dealing with a wide variety of family, social, and health topics.

Remarried Parents, Inc.
  Box 323
  Times Square Station
  New York, N.Y. 10036
  Organization for stepparents and remarried divorcés.

Sex Information and Education Council of the U.S. (SIECUS)
  1855 Broadway
  New York, N.Y. 10023
  Source for information on sex education.

United States Department of Health, Education, and Welfare
  Washington, D.C. 20201

  Children's Bureau, Welfare Administration, and Public Health Service provide information on child-rearing, parent education, family life, and health; publications available from U.S. Government Printing Office, Washington D.C. 20402

Your local librarian can provide a wealth of information about reading on general and special topics for you and your children.

BOOKS

On Fathers and Fatherhood

Benson, Leonard. *Fatherhood: a Sociological Perspective*. New York: Random House, Inc., 1968.

  Well-written comprehensive text providing in-depth background on fathering. Excellent bibliography.

Biller, Henry B. *Father, Child, and Sex Role*. Lexington, Mass.: Heath-Lexington Books, 1971.

Scholarly summary of the author's and others' research on the psychological functions of fathers. Bibliography.

Biller, Henry B., and Meredith, Dennis. *Father Power*. New York: David McKay Company, Inc., 1974.

A psychologist who has specialized in the father/child relationship looks at fatherhood.

Dodson, Fitzhugh, M.D. *How to Father*. Los Angeles: Nash Publishing, 1973.

By the author of *How to Parent,* a writer with usually good ideas and generally strong opinions.

English, O. Spurgeon, M.D., and Foster, Constance J. *Fathers Are Parents, Too*. New York: G. P. Putnam's Sons, 1951.

An older book with still-useful insights.

Klein, Ted. *The Father's Book*. New York: William Morrow & Co., Inc., 1968.

A thick book with some useful advice and some specifics on "male-interest" topics.

Schaefer, George, M.D. *Expectant Father*. New York: Barnes & Noble, 1972.

An obstetrician writes for the "other parent."

On Child Development and Psychology

Albrecht, Margaret. *Parents and Teenagers: Getting Through to Each Other*. New York: Parents' Magazine Press, 1972.

A thoughtful book on the problems and achievements of adolescence. Bibliography.

Association for Childhood Education International. *Feelings and Learning*. Washington: Association for Childhood Education International, 1965.

On emotional development.

Beadle, Muriel. *A Child's Mind*. New York: Doubleday, 1970.

A clear and well-written account of how the mind develops and how children learn during the crucial early years.

Erikson, Erik H. *Childhood and Society*. New York: W. W. Norton & Co., 1963.

Parts One and Three of this classic offer especially good analyses of emotional and psychological growth from birth into adulthood.

Fraiberg, Selma. *The Magic Years*. New York: Charles Scribner's Sons, 1959.

Warm, witty, good reading about psychological and emotional growth during the first six years, by an experienced psychoanalyst.

Gardner, George E., M.D., and others. *The Emerging Personality: Infancy through Adolescence*. New York: Delacorte, 1970.

A comprehensive discussion of growth of the personality from birth through adolescence.

Gesell, Arnold, M.D., and Ilg, Frances, M.D. *Infant and Child in the Culture of Today*. New York: Harper & Row Publishers, Inc., 1943.
————. *The Child from Five to Ten*. New York: Harper & Row Publishers, Inc., 1946.
————, and Ames, Louise Bates. *Youth: The Years from Ten to Sixteen*, New York: Harper and Row Publishers, Inc., 1956.

These pioneering studies still provide useful information and contain charts for quick reference.

Gilbert, Sara D. *Three Years to Grow*. New York: Parents' Magazine Press, 1972.

On the first three years of life.

Gruenberg, Sidonie Matson. *The Parents' Guide to Everyday Problems of Boys and Girls*. New York: Random House, Inc., 1958.

A guide for the "middle years" by a wise authority.

Hoover, Mary B. *The Responsive Parent*. New York: Parents' Magazine Press, 1972.

Informative advice for the challenges of parenthood. Bibliography.

Josselyn, Irene M., M.D. *Adolescence*. New York: Harper & Row Publishers, Inc., 1971

A useful discussion of the topic (published under the auspices of the Joint Commission of Mental Health for Children), but addressed more to the professional than the lay person.

Minton, Lynn. *Growing into Adolescence*. New York: Parents' Magazine Press, 1972.

A practical guide to the years from 11 to 14. Bibliography.

Mogal, Doris P. *Character in the Making*. New York: Parents' Magazine Press, 1972.

Sensible advice about the school-aged child. Bibliography.

Smart, Mollie and Russell. *Child Development and Relationships*. New York: The Macmillan Co., 1972.

In textbook format, a clear and understandable description of the various areas of development.

Spock, Benjamin, M.D. *Baby and Child Care*. New York: Pocket Books, 1974.

In the back of the book are thumbnail sketches of growth and behavior at different ages and stages.

On Marriage Today

Bernard, Jessie. *The Future of Marriage*. New York: World Publishing Co., 1972

A thoughtful book about people's changing needs and marriage's changing forms.

Folkman, Jerome D., and Clatworthy, Nancy M. K. *Marriage Has Many Faces*. Columbus, Ohio: Charles E. Merrill, 1970.

A textbook with many good ideas.

O'Neill, Nena and George. *Open Marriage*. Philadelphia: J. P. Lippincott Co., 1971.

Parts of this are pop, parts are naive, but overall it is an intelligent guide for those interested in flexing their lives.

Peterson, James A. *Married Love in the Middle Years*. New York: Association Press, 1968.

A marriage counselor offers guidance to the older parent.

Rapoport, Rhona and Robert. *Dual-Career Families*. England: Penguin Books Ltd., 1971.

Case studies of British working couples with children and their family life-styles.

Rogers, Carl R. *Becoming Partners: Marriage and Its Alternatives*. New York: Delacorte Press, 1972.

A psychotherapist explores the process of marriage. Bibliography.

Skolnick, Arlene S., and Jerome H. *Family in Transition*. Boston: Little, Brown and Co., 1971

A collection of ideas on changing family life.

On Divorce and Single-Parenthood

Decker, Beatrice, and Korman, Gladys. *After the Flowers Have Gone*. Grand Rapids, Mich.: Vondervan Publishing House, 1973.

Primarily for widows, but with some value to widowers.

Despert, J. Louise, M.D. *Children of Divorce*. New York: Doubleday & Co., Inc., 1953.

Classic explores impact of divorcing—and staying together—on children.

Egleson, Jim, and Egleson, Janet Frank. *Parents Without Partners*. New York: E. P. Dutton & Co., 1961.

A sensible guide for divorcing, divorced, and single parents.

Epstein, Joseph. *Divorced in America—Marriage in an Age of Possibility*. New York: E. P. Dutton & Co., 1974.

A divorced father shares his difficult personal experience and offers thoughts on modern marriage.

Gardner, Richard. *The Boys and Girls Book about Divorce*. New York: Jason Aronson, 1970.

Recommended by authorities and by divorced parents as an excellent explanation and talk-starter about divorce.

Goff, Beth. *Where Is Daddy?* Boston: Beacon Press, 1969.

Another reassuring book for children about divorce.

Groffman, Earl A. *Explaining Divorce to Children*. Boston: Beacon Press, 1972.

A sensible, sensitive guide.

Hunt, Morton L. *The World of the Formerly Married*. New York: McGraw-Hill, Inc., 1966.

Some good insights into fatherhood with and without custody.

Klein, Carole. *The Single Parent Experience*. New York: Walker Publishing Co., Inc., 1973

Some interesting ideas on raising children without benefit of female.

Krantzler, Mel. *Creative Divorce*. New York: M. Evans & Co., Inc., 1973.

Looking on the bright side of a tough situation.

Lyman, Howard B. *Single Again*. New York: David McKay Co., Inc., 1971.

Some ideas on coping with freedom.

Sheresky, Norman, and Mannes, Marya. *Uncoupling*. New York: The Viking Press, Inc., 1972.

Some intelligent thoughts on creative divorce.

Sherwin, Robert V. *Compatible Divorce*. New York: Crown Publishers, 1969.

A lawyer offers practical advice for divorcing couples.

Thomson, Helen. *The Successful Stepparent*. New York: Harper & Row Publishers, Inc., 1966.

Sensible thoughts on how to "marry" a family.

On Sex Education and Venereal Disease

Arnstein, Helene. *Your Growing Child and Sex*. New York: Bobbs-Merrill Co., Inc., 1967.

A parents' guide to the physical, social, and emotional aspects of sexual development, from birth through adolescence.

Bohannon, Paul. *Love, Sex, and Being Human*. New York: Doubleday, 1969.

For young adults, an explanation of the physiological changes of puberty and an exploration of many aspects of sexuality.

Demarest, Robert, and Sciarra, John J., M.D. *Conception, Birth, and Contraception*. New York: McGraw-Hill, Inc., 1969.

A factual presentation for adults or teens.

Grover, John W., M.D., and Grace, Dick. *VD: The ABC's*. Englewood Cliffs, N.J.: Prentice-Hall Co., 1970.

The basic facts about venereal disease.

Gruenberg, Sidonie Matson. *The Wonderful Story of How You Were Born*. New York: Doubleday, 1970.

An honest, sensitive guide for parents and their younger children.

Johnson, Eric W. *Sex: Telling It Straight*. Philadelphia: J. B. Lippincott Co., 1970.

A good book for the junior-high group.

Rosebury, Theodor. *Microbes and Morals*. New York: The Viking Press, Inc., 1971.

A fascinating and factual book about venereal disease.

SIECUS. *Sexuality and Man*. New York: Charles Scribner's Sons, 1970.

A collection of papers on many aspects of sex gathered by the Sex Information and Education Council of the US.

Wood, Frederic C., Jr. *Sex and the New Morality*. New York: The Association Press, 1968.

A college chaplain explores changing mores for young people and their parents.

Yale University Student Committee on Human Sexuality. *The Student Guide to Sex on Campus*. New York: New American Library, 1970.

Forthright facts about sex and sexuality.

On Drugs

Ayars, Albert L., and Milgram, Gail G. *The Teenager and Alcohol*. New York: Richards Rosen Press, 1970.

Brief, clear presentation for teens about drinking.

Child Study Association. *You, Your Child and Drugs*. New York: Child Study, 1971.

Presentation of facts plus exploration of attitudes and situations causing and accompanying drug abuse.

Gorodetzky, Charles W., and Christian, Samuel T. *What You Should Know About Drugs*. New York: Harcourt, Brace, Jovanovich, 1970.

A sensible presentation for preteens and teens.

Greenberg, Harvey R., M.D. *What You Must Know About Drugs*. New York: Scholastic Press, 1970.

The facts for teens, calmly and readably.

Madison, Arnold. *Drugs and You*. New York: Julian Messner, 1971.

Drug facts presented simply for preteens.

Whitney, Elizabeth D. *Living with Alcoholism*. Boston: Beacon Press, 1968.

A guide to alcoholism and its treatment.

Index

Sara D. Gilbert is a writer and the mother of a small boy with whose help—and despite whose assistance—she managed to write her first popularly acclaimed book, THREE YEARS TO GROW—Guidance for Your Child's First Three Years, published by Parents' Magazine Press in 1972. A native of Washington, D.C. she is a graduate of Barnard College and has written extensively on law and social problems.

James Stevenson, an artist and writer for *The New Yorker* since 1956, has written three novels, several children's books and has illustrated others. He and his wife and children live in Connecticut.

MUST READING FOR ALL PARENTS!

WHAT EVERY CHILD WOULD LIKE HIS PARENTS TO KNOW
(78-160, $1.50)

by Dr. Lee Salk

Dr. Lee Salk offers common-sense guidelines for answering children's questions on such subjects as sex, divorce, death, brothers and sisters, discipline, sleep, homework and stealing. Here is a book that belongs next to Dr. Spock on all family library shelves.

HOW TO RAISE A HUMAN BEING

by Dr. Lee Salk and Rita Kramer **(78-922, $1.50)**

A guide to help meet your youngster's needs and help him grow. The authors believe you can prevent troubles before they start by understanding how a child develops and being ready to cope, without pressure or anxiety, with each stage as it comes along.

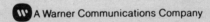 A Warner Communications Company

- -

Please send me the books I have checked.

Enclose check or money order only, no cash please. Plus 35¢ per copy to cover postage and handling. N.Y. State residents add applicable sales tax.

Please allow 2 weeks for delivery.

WARNER BOOKS
P.O. Box 690
New York, N. Y. 10019

Name...

Address..

City .... State .... Zip ....

_____ Please send me your free mail order catalog

REQUIRED READING FOR PARENTS

HOW TO SURVIVE PARENTHOOD
by By Eda LeShan   **(76-143 / $1.25)**
At last, a book that puts joy back into raising a family! A book that caters to the needs of **parents**—as couples and individuals—and not just the demands of children. **Must** reading for enlightened mothers and fathers.

SEX AND YOUR TEENAGER
by Eda LeShan   **(76-204 / $1.25)**
Noted family counselor, TV lecturer and authority on youth, Eda LeShan takes a very candid and forthright look at how parents can cope with their teenagers and a rapidly changing morality.

W A Warner Communications Company

- -

Please send me the books I have checked.

Enclose check or money order only, no cash please. Plus 35¢ per copy to cover postage and handling. N.Y. State residents add applicable sales tax.

Please allow 2 weeks for delivery.

WARNER BOOKS
P.O. Box 690
New York, N.Y. 10019

Name. . . . .

Address. . . . .

City . . . . State . . . . Zip . . . .

_____ Please send me your free mail order catalog

THE BEST OF BESTSELLERS
FROM WARNER BOOKS!

WITHOUT FEATHERS by Woody Allen   **(89-035, $1.95)**
A major N.Y. Times bestseller; Woody Allen's funniest book since **Getting Even.** This new collection of short pieces and plays "crackles with droll remarks... mixing the comic with the cosmic"— **Hartford Courant**

ALL THE PRESIDENT'S MEN   **(79-732, $1.95)**
by Carl Bernstein and Bob Woodward
The #1 Bestseller! Now a Major Motion Picture! "A classic in the art of political reportage."—**New York Times** "Brilliant—a success on a number of levels, not the least among them the level of a political thriller."—**Atlantic Monthly**

LOVE'S TENDER FURY by Jennifer Wilde   **(79-921, $1.95)**
A big historical romance a la Rosemary Rogers that magnificently depicts the early years of our country as well as the fascinating life of a beautiful and turbulent woman.

JOURNEY by Robert and Suzanne Massie   **(89-049, $1.95)**
Robert Massie, bestselling author of **Nicholas and Alexandra,** and his wife Suzanne relive their 18-year struggle against their only son's hemophilia. With 8 pages of photographs, this is an inspiring story of how a boy has been helped to live a full and productive life against overwhelming odds.

 A Warner Communications Company

- -

Please send me the books I have checked.

Enclose check or money order only, no cash please. Plus 35¢ per copy to cover postage and handling. N.Y. State residents add applicable sales tax.

Please allow 2 weeks for delivery.

WARNER BOOKS
P.O. Box 690
New York, N.Y. 10019

Name...

Address..

City .... State .... Zip ......

_____ Please send me your free mail order catalog